New Minimalism

New Minimalism

Decluttering and Design for
Sustainable, Intentional Living

CARY TELANDER FORTIN
+ KYLE LOUISE QUILICI

Photography by Kelly Ishikawa

SASQUATCH BOOKS
SEATTLE

For Cam and Brady

Printed in China

Published by Sasquatch Books

22 21 20 19 18   9 8 7 6 5 4 3 2 1

Editor: Hannah Elnan | Production editor: Bridget Sweet
Design: Anna Goldstein | Copyeditor: Janice Lee
Photographer: Kelly Ishikawa
Contributing photographers: Sarah Deragon (pages 4, 11, 17, 72, 77, 85, 90, 196), Anna-Alexia Basile (pages 94, 176), Ryan James Devisser (pages 34, 43, 124, 146, 153, bottom of 161, 165)

Library of Congress Cataloging-in-Publication Data
Names: Fortin, Cary Telander, author. | Quilici, Kyle Louise, author.
Title: New minimalism : decluttering and design for sustainable,
    intentional living / Cary Telander Fortin and Kyle Louise Quilici.
Description: Seattle : Sasquatch Books, [2018]
Identifiers: LCCN 2017028684 | ISBN 9781632171320 (hardcover)
Subjects: LCSH: Storage in the home. | House cleaning. | Orderliness.
Classification: LCC TX324 .F667 2018 | DDC 648/.8--dc23
LC record available at https://lccn.loc.gov/2017028684

ISBN: 978-1-63217-132-0

Sasquatch Books
1904 Third Avenue, Suite 710 | Seattle, WA 98101
(206) 467-4300 | custserv@sasquatchbooks.com
www.sasquatchbooks.com

The names and other identifying characteristics used throughout this book have been changed to ensure the privacy of our beloved clients.

CONTENTS

INTRODUCTION

New Minimalism is a call to a mindful, intentional way of living, prioritizing relationships and experiences above material things. It's a way of life celebrating the idea that you can't buy your happiness. This philosophy maintains that your time is better spent experiencing life with people than it is spent looking for, managing, organizing, cleaning, and purchasing (and subsequently returning) things.

Traditional minimalism worships at the altar of *less is better*. It is an austere philosophy of stripping down to the bare essentials and questioning what is required for one's basic survival. It conjures imagery of ascetic, Thoreau-like solitude: owning a single fork and knife while foraging berries from the surrounding woods. While living under these extreme conditions certainly provides valuable lessons, over time it can be constricting and limiting.

At the opposite end of the spectrum is the consumer-based lifestyle that has unfortunately become synonymous with the American Dream. This hyperconsumption was exciting at first (read: all cultural evidence from the '80s). But then we came to collectively understand there was a weight and heaviness associated with all this stuff. And living this way was not only constricting us on an individual basis but was also harming our beautiful planet.

New Minimalism exists as a middle path between traditional minimalism and over-the-top consumerism. We honor the vital role material things have in our lives. We appreciate beauty, textures, and color in our homes. We know the joy of a favorite mug; we understand the comfortable embrace of a loved sweater. We savor art that lacks a practical purpose yet speaks volumes to our souls. And we believe that the beauty of these favorite items is elevated against a quiet backdrop. Our approach is not prescriptive or formulaic; you won't have to catalog everything you own or whittle your possessions down to a specific number of items. This book is about finding your own wonderful, decidedly unique middle path.

On this middle path we seek out what the Swedish call *lagom*. This word is often translated as "enough"; however, it is far more nuanced and lovely than that. A closer definition is "just the right amount." Perhaps the most important thing to recognize about *lagom* is that by definition it is subjective. There is beauty in all its flexibility, in knowing that *lagom* doesn't inherently mean two bath towels per person any more than it means eight. It means the amount that is right for you at this time, in this life.

"Wait," you may ask, "so does that mean I can keep all forty of my pairs of boots?" Well, no, not exactly. The challenge is to reach this place of *lagom* while concurrently cultivating a spaciousness in your home and in your days. Defining what *lagom* means to you requires a return to your true, basic self. You have to remove years of programming and hundreds of thousands of advertisements; you have to look past what the people around you are doing and perhaps even reject the way in which you were raised. You have to get very quiet and deeply honest with yourself. Only then will you know what *lagom* means for you. Consider this book your guide.

THE BENEFITS

Before we dig into the hows behind decluttering and redesigning your home the New Minimalist way, it's important to know the whys. Below are just a few of the benefits you can expect from your newly simplified life.

- *Actual* free time. When you have less to buy, to clean, to maintain, you finally get to relax and have that down time. You get to be that person you see in magazines who is simply reading on the couch or making a lively meal with his kids.
- Money saved. You have fewer things to buy and fewer things

to fix when they break. You save money, which allows you to invest in things made of higher quality and durability. It's a cycle of prosperity.
- **Fewer to-dos.** This basically results in more sanity, which we could all use, right?
- **Room for spontaneity.** When you intentionally agree to only the most important and fulfilling time commitments and say no to the rest, you leave space in your schedule to say yes to a spontaneous date or to pop into that lecture at the community center.

A NOBLE ACT OF ENVIRONMENTALISM

There are a number of other significant yet less obvious benefits to cultivating a simpler life, like, ahem, saving the planet! Minimalism is inherently a form of environmental activism. Whether or not being a warrior for our planet's health was at the top of your to-do list when you picked up this book, when you adopt the habits we discuss here, your actions will be a benevolent service to our earth.

As a follower of New Minimalism, you choose to buy less overall with a focus on purchasing quality, long-lasting goods. When you spend less time shopping at malls and online, when you redefine your consumption habits to support your pure needs and selected wants, you are, in a small but significant way, decreasing demand for the manufacture of new items. As a result, you are treading far more gently on this earth while graciously sharing its resources with your greater community.

Committing to owning fewer, better things means that you have more time to purchase intentionally; you can take the time to source a Forest Stewardship Council–certified dining table or wait for the perfect lamp to arrive at the consignment shop. Since you're purchasing less, you can use the money you save to support fair-trade and locally made goods. In turn, you'll have quality items that last longer, and you'll be promoting an ethos of production that benefits yourself; the workers, farmers, and craftspeople who made each item; and the environment.

SERVE OUR COMMUNITIES

At New Minimalism, we take a stand when it comes to disposing of the items we declutter: first and foremost we donate everything we can. By taking the extra time and energy to find organizations that can use items our clients no longer need, we are doing a world of good for our environment and we are giving back to the communities that support and sustain us.

If items can't be donated, we first try to compost them, then we look to see if they are recyclable, and then—when there are no other options available—we throw items away. We ask you to commit to the ethos of giving generously, to make this promise ahead of time knowing that it will take a little extra work on your end. If enough of us commit to living simply and generously, we can alter the future of our planet, leaving it healthier and our communities more connected than we found them.

CULTIVATE MINDFULNESS

If you've ever received meditation guidance, you were probably instructed to quiet the chatter in your mind and settle into the experience of breathing and observing rather than attaching or reacting to your catalog of never-ending thoughts. These skills of quieting and centering are the exact skills our style of decluttering will have you tap into and strengthen.

We ask you to move beyond the fears, anxieties, and reactions in order to sink into a deeper, quieter place of knowing. In decluttering your home, you have the opportunity—in fact, thousands of micro-opportunities—to strengthen and deepen your mindfulness and to incorporate this into your everyday life. To be clear, this is not a frantic desire to organize, clean, and be made "better" but the chance to tap into your underlying self who has always been there, the one who knows what you truly need and wholeheartedly love.

SEPARATE YOUR IDENTITY FROM YOUR THINGS

Our stuff has become a kind of placeholder for the type of people we think we should be. A loving mom should bake fresh bread for her family. A successful career man should wear this type of clothing. A well-educated woman should read and own these books.

This is often the biggest part of the discourse when decluttering: releasing who we think we should be and embracing the fullest, truest, most loving version of who we actually are. This might entail acknowledging that as a working parent, you might not have the time or energy to bake a weekly loaf of bread. Or that those jeans from college are actually just a subtle, not-so-kind reminder of the waist size you used to be. Or that just because your father read *War and Peace* doesn't mean you also have to.

By releasing the baking supplies you never seem to use, the jeans stashed at the back of your closet, the dusty books on the shelf, you are embracing your life as it is today. You are separating your identity from your things, proclaiming that you are not defined by them. And let us tell you, this is so deeply liberating.

DO THE WORK

Like most things in life, meaningful change does not result from cutting corners. You can't just skip to the end. No one can do this for you.

If you find that this process feels easy, it's likely because you've done a lot of hard work leading up to this point. You've changed and altered and questioned and felt a little lost and then found yourself. You may have made it through a big transition. If you find this process deeply challenging, that is because your habits and thought patterns are still realigning. Both of these are okay.

Above all, we want for you what you want for yourself. There is no perfect number of socks to own; there is no specific aesthetic which is better than another, no type of hobby that a minimalist ought to partake in. As one of our favorite sayings goes, "You do you." Own your life. Celebrate it. Make it beautiful, make it inspiring, and make it work for you.

PART I:

The Philosophy

We've discovered that owning things
and consuming things does not
satisfy our longing for meaning.
We've learned that piling up material
goods cannot fill the emptiness
of lives which have no confidence
or purpose. —*Jimmy Carter*

CHAPTER 1

Laying the Foundation

We met in perhaps the most California way possible: carpooling from our apartments in San Francisco to a weekend yoga retreat in the mountains of Ojai. Right away, we bonded over our matching early-'90s Ford Explorers (while Kyle's was still running, Cary reminisced about her "Exploder," which had just passed on to the scrap yard). Twenty minutes in, we laughed about how we'd both bartered and found ways to go on this retreat for free. Less than an hour into our drive south, we were knee-deep in philosophies of sustainability, living simply, and the connection between the two.

It was the spring of 2011, and without knowing one another, we'd been walking parallel, if quirky, paths on our way to distilling a desire for living kindly, simply, and mindfully into a functional lifestyle. Cary had recently stepped away from a career in corporate law and was cutting her personal consumption habits as a result. She was experimenting in all ways possible to find the boundary between what was too little and what was enough in order to reach a place of financial freedom. Kyle, on the other hand, had been studying the intersection of sustainability and interior design. She knew there was a way to improve interior spaces without the traditional approach of buy, buy, buy.

Even though we arrived at minimalism from different backgrounds, we connected most over a shared epiphany. Prior to

embarking on our paths of these new lifestyles, we had each held the belief that simplicity was synonymous with sacrifice and discomfort. We thought that cutting back on the hyper-consumption of the culture surrounding us would feel restricting, limiting, and like we were missing out. But once we actually started to employ these practices, we were blown away by the litany of positive side effects. We had more time, we saved more money, we had flexibility within our schedules, we developed more meaningful relationships. What we had thought would be painful and uncomfortable was instead liberating and joyful. We were experiencing peace of mind.

After the retreat, we promised to stay in touch. After all, how often do you meet your philosophical soul mate while sitting in California highway traffic? Of course, back in the city, real life resumed, and we were each sucked back into our work and personal lives. Apparently the universe decided to give us one more shot, though: we literally ran into each other on Fillmore Street in San Francisco a few months later. Maybe it was something about our second chance encounter, about remembering that there was another person in this big city with these same weird ideas, but this time it stuck. We committed then and there to meet for coffee every other month to share ideas and inspiration. Kyle would share her favorite sustainable-design websites, mindfulness books, and vegetarian recipes. Cary would share the piles of new books she'd checked out from the library on simple living, personal growth, and decision making.

We kept wondering: Why hadn't anyone ever told us about this concept of minimalism before? Why didn't more people know about this amazing secret we'd stumbled upon? And why was our entire society geared toward supporting the *opposite* as being true—that material acquisition and the pursuit of money, power, and position equate to happiness? Like any great discovery, it became our mission to share this lifestyle with the world.

We boiled it down to helping others remove the excess. We began to work out our decluttering methodology by practicing on open and willing friends who either had expressed frustration with their things or lived in spaces that we saw had great potential. With each carload of donations we brought to a local church or a women's shelter or an elementary school, we felt our hearts grow. With each friend that we left with a simplified, inspiring home came deep feelings of satisfaction.

And then, as the weeks went by and these same clients told us about the big life changes they'd made—the new partners who had entered into their lives, their new passion for living with minimal waste, their newfound comfort in their homes—we knew that we had found our sweet spot. We'd created for our-selves a job that helped others and aligned with our passion for the environment, all while creating intentional and beautiful spaces. We get to make hard things easier. To lighten burdens, to lift spirits, to open space for happiness and creativity. We find it an honor to bear witness to the things that people part with, to celebrate their rediscovery of an item they deeply love, to support them through the challenges of the process, and to shepherd them into a new phase in their lives.

Cary's most recent move to Boise, Idaho, expanded our base of readers and clients and also brought about another level of growth in our philosophy. Her new house was significantly larger than the one-bedroom apartment she'd shared with her husband, Cam, for six years. As such, Kyle and Cary began dis-cussing a new set of questions: How does a minimalist live well when space is no longer restricted? How do those of us who live in suburbs or more rural areas connect with donation partners? How do we view our things knowing they might actually be more challenging to replace than by just walking down a city block with a vast selection of stores? How do we keep our elevated stan-dards for what enters our lives when there is plenty of room? This move expanded and deepened our understanding of mini-malism across geographic lines.

DECLUTTERING VERSUS ORGANIZING

While many aspects of our process developed over time and through practice, there is one condition that we knew from the very inception of New Minimalism: we are not home organiz-ers. Let us repeat: this book is not about organization. In our process we first and foremost *declutter*, and we will tell you why this distinction matters.

A home organizer will take all your worldly possessions and perfectly organize, color-code, and alphabetize them. At New Minimalism, however, we have you question whether those items

should even be there in the first place. A perfectly organized space does not automatically mean you lead an effortless, clutter-free life. In fact, the need for a complicated organizational system is usually indicative of too much stuff to begin with. A beautiful, easy-to-maintain, organized home is simply one of many positive by-products of a thoughtfully curated and decluttered life.

When in pursuit of restoring order to your home, look not to the big-box home organizing stores and magazines for answers. Their solutions beckon with promises of order and free time. But in reality, most of those multicolored stacking plastic drawers are where your things go to die. Once you finally haul those drawers home and neatly tuck away all your doodads, those items are now out of sight, out of mind, and pretty much guaranteed to never be engaged with again. How sad!

Effortful and intricate organization systems are entirely against the greater point of having your things work for you. Complicated systems require time and money to obtain, effort to install, and constant energy to keep up. Be wary of any system that requires a significant amount of your time to maintain. Do you really want to spend an hour of your precious Saturday afternoon maintaining your recipe archives or your tool shed? All for a system that is supposedly making things easier for you? We didn't think so. And as such we always default to the simplest, easiest systems possible.

If you were looking for the can opener in Cary's kitchen, it would be in the one drawer designated for kitchen tools. That's it. No labeled slot the can opener must be returned to. It's just in the drawer with the six or so other tools she uses all the time. Similarly, Kyle corrals her pajamas in a small basket in her closet. Sometimes the clothes are folded; sometimes they are floating free. But what allows this version of contained chaos to work is the fact that there are few items in the basket to begin with.

ORGANIZATION CAN BE EASY

Imagine two different closets. The first is packed full with clothing. Clothes are stacked dozens high on every shelf; they spill out of drawers and share hangers with other items of clothing. Sure, there are many options of things to wear. But how accessible are those options? And how much time does it take to find exactly what you are looking for? And what emotions do you experience when you try to grab a pair of pants and nine others fall onto the floor, or when you can't remember where you hung something up, whether it's dirty, or what pile it might be in or under?

Now imagine a second closet. It looks like the inside of a curated clothing boutique. Each item is elegantly draped from its own hanger. The hangers are spaced so that every garment can be seen and each hanger can be easily grabbed. Folded clothing exists in manageable stacks three or four items tall. A couple of scarves live loose in a bin, and a week's worth of undershirts are casually placed in their own drawer.

The second closet does not have more space than the first. It does not have complicated racks installed for shoes, nor does it have pants stored on elaborate, multitiered hanger systems. There are no specialty wall-mounted bins to hold a collection of evening clutches nor airtight bags for confining voluminous sweaters. The primary difference between the two closets is the quantity of items inside.

The same exact closet that seems hopelessly overwhelming, cramped, and dark can be made to feel light, elegant, and accessible simply by reducing the number of items you attempt to store inside. We've seen it happen hundreds of times. When the number of items in an area suits the space, you will find that organization simply emerges.

Evolutionarily speaking, it used to be in our best interest to hold on to things as they came into our lives: resources were rare and could be the difference between surviving or dying. This reality changed with the advent of the Industrial Revolution, when all varieties of goods became cheaper and more readily available to the masses. We had life-changing new inventions like the dishwasher, the washing machine, and cars—what more could we want? Not much. What we wanted was to enjoy and savor this newfound leisure time. And as a result, consumption of goods began to slow.

Fast-forward to World War II, and this consumer contentment was now at odds with our new economy. As economist Victor Lebow noted in his 1955 article for the *Journal of Retailing*, "Our enormously productive economy demands that we make consumption our way of life." So how did we transition from content people whose needs were being met to overconsumers of things we don't need? Enter our modern-day big-budget multimedia advertising industry.

Today, to keep the wheels of consumption turning, advertising companies not only hire the brightest business minds and spend billions of dollars convincing us to buy things we don't need but also employ a sneaky technique called *neuromarketing*. With the help of neuroscientists, advertisers can now tap into both our conscious and unconscious brain to override our natural circuitry, which would normally tell us that we are content and that we have enough.

Instead, advertisements trigger our reptilian brain and make us feel that we are lacking something. And then, once we are in this vulnerable place, we are conveniently presented with the item that will solve this "problem." Oh dear, you eat food? You probably suffer from bad breath. It's likely the reason you never seem to find a relationship. Here, try this mouthwash to attract your soul mate!

With New Minimalism, we ask you to pause and reevaluate your previously reactive buying habits. Now every thoughtful purchase—and nonpurchase—is an act of rebellion, a declaration to businesses and advertisers that you are not merely a passive consumer purchasing according to their advertising calendar and quarterly financial forecasts. Your purchasing power is one part of this wild and unpredictable life that you *can* control. We encourage you to exercise this right.

QUESTION
EVERYTHING

- Work until you are sixty-five.
- Upgrade your phone, computer, and TV as soon as you have space on your credit card.
- Save 5 percent of your annual income.
- Buy as big a house as your mortgage lender says you can afford.
- Treat yourself to luxury goods and services—you've worked so hard, you deserve it.
- Buy your kids the newest toys for each birthday and holiday—that's how you show love.
- Constantly revamp your wardrobe—you need to keep up with the newest trends.

The above messages are sent to us constantly via advertising, but they're also taught to us in school and pervade most news sources. When we're continually fed these opinions, they gain the weight of fact; they seem unavoidable, inalterable.

By living simple lives, we learn that these messages just aren't true. You get to choose your life, and you get to decide how you spend your time and your money.

And while the assumptions above may seem reasonable enough, there is something maleficent lurking below the surface. When enough people begin to say something is impossible (saving 71 percent of your income, not producing any trash, retiring at thirty), it begins to seem true. And when things seem impossible, we begin to give away our power, believing we cannot control what we own, how we spend our time or money, or how we use our space.

The first thing we do with our clients is get an understanding of how they want to feel in their space and the values they would like their home to support. We cannot walk in and say, "Get rid of this plate" or "You must keep that painting," because we know that every person, family, and home is unique.

After this introductory fact-finding, we assess each and every item with fresh eyes, determining whether it should stay or be donated based on how well it serves those values and desires.

The first step is always the same: question everything. By this we mean start from a place of compassionate curiosity and question everything that you've brought into your life so far. Ask yourself a new type of question, like "Can I live without this?" or "Does this really bring me happiness?" or "Is this something that I am actively choosing for myself or just something that I've always had?" This helps you to start from scratch without any limitations or beliefs about what you should have or want. Instead, you dream up your own ideal future and then reconstruct your space with that vision in mind.

OUR DEFINITION OF *CLUTTER*

In order to declutter, it's probably best to have a clear understanding of what clutter is. Dictionary.com defines *clutter* as "a disorderly heap or assemblage." Based on this definition, one might presume that an *organized* heap or assemblage is no longer considered clutter. We have seen dozens of organized and orderly spaces that are still full of clutter. Others might tell you that it's not clutter if it gives you extreme happiness or joy. But we've found that subjective definitions of *joy* can be a slippery slope and can be used to justify keeping your fifteenth super-cute swimsuit. Others believe that clutter begins only after you hit "x" number of items. The prescriptive definitions of *clutter* are wide and varied, and we don't agree with any of them.

Now, Peter Walsh, Oprah's organization guru, defines *clutter* as "anything that stands between you and the vision you have for your best life." OK, this definition is getting warmer. We believe that *clutter* is best defined individually and situationally. Through questioning everything, people get to determine how they want to feel in a space (for example, joyful, calm, or inspired) and their own lifestyle needs and desires. The material items that *don't* support this vision are clutter.

THE EQUATION IS OUT OF BALANCE

When was the last time you brought a new possession into your home? Maybe it was an article of clothing, a piece of decor, or something small like a new mug or a set of pens. Today, possibly. Maybe yesterday. Almost certainly this week.

For the typical American, a new item enters the home almost *daily*. An Amazon package arriving at your doorstep with a new book or a quick dash into a store for a pair of shoes has shockingly turned into a part of everyday life for a lot of people. Add to this the half-dozen life events when we are showered with gifts, and is it any surprise that the average American household contains three hundred thousand items?

Now recall the last time you let go of an item because you simply didn't enjoy it or need it anymore. When was the last time you released *several* bags or boxes of items all at once without replacing them with something new? For many people, it's likely been years or even decades. Or perhaps you've never completed a big purge in your entire life. Our culture's big clutter problem is not only due to new stuff constantly crossing the threshold of our homes but also the great infrequency with which things leave our homes. If you're good at math, it's pretty simple: the equation is out of balance.

HIT THE RESET BUTTON

A popular decluttering strategy we've seen some of our clients test out before calling us in is the "one a day" method of donating one item daily. Despite diligently sticking to their plan, these clients become frustrated when they find that this daily practice has barely made a dent in their space. Other clients practice the "one in, one out" rule, meaning that anytime new things enter their home, they have to get rid of an equal number of items. They, too, end up feeling as though they are running in place, always dealing with their items but never making any noticeable progress. This is because both of these theories are excellent, but only for maintaining an already decluttered home.

In order to get to that place of pure maintenance, you first have to hit the reset button and complete one huge, sweeping clear-out. You have to deal with the backlog of items that have accumulated in order to get to a point where you are simply maintaining a clutter-free space. This big reset is not a type of self-flagellation or asceticism, or the cause of deep suffering. It is in fact the opposite. It's a skimming of the fat, a removing of the excess so that what is needed and used and loved has the space and attention it deserves.

In life's great ecosystem, envision yourself as a "leverage point." This is a term coined by the environmental educator Donella Meadows for "places within a complex system (a corporation, an economy, a living body, a city, an ecosystem) where a small shift in one thing can produce big changes in everything." As you tread lightly, mindfully, and generously, picture the ripple effect of your actions as they radiate out from your home, into your community, until eventually they encompass this little blue dot called Earth that we all share.

WHAT'S MOST IMPORTANT TO YOU?

On the surface, we help people declutter and design their spaces. But what we really do is guide overwhelmed, fatigued folks through a process of peeling back layers (of stuff, commitments, habits, or beliefs) until they have clarity about what matters most to them. We have found that people who have recently undergone a major life transition, those who have experienced a deep shift from what used to be to what now is, tend to have the clearest vision for what is important in life. They appreciate the profound clarity that comes with grief, change, sickness, divorce, or death. At this point, what we believe we need versus what we really need reveals itself in a pure way. Stuff is worth little, if anything at all, when we are stripped bare in front of life's big events.

It's typical for our clients to hit roadblocks in our sessions. As the morning's coffee fades and they sit surrounded by all the stuff that they've chosen to bring into their lives, clients often struggle with deciding what should stay and what should go. They're adrift in a sea of thoughts, ruminating on why they should keep something, why it came into their lives to begin with, and how much they gave up in order to have it.

This is where considering the brevity of life is so valuable. Trying to sort through a million potential futures in order to determine whether an item should stay ("I might need this someday if . . .") is a herculean task. However, armed with the awareness that life is short, we are instantly called back to our cores, to the very center of what matters.

From this place our clients can step back and say, "Oh, *this* is what matters to me: how I spend my days, how I feel when I first open my eyes in the morning, how I respond to the cries of my child, how much mental clarity I need in order to take care of myself. Which of my things help me do that?"

When clients have this realization, the extraneous stuff goes flying out the door. Spare bathrobes, old shin guards, extra pots and pans, old paperwork, unfinished projects—what are these objects other than things that are blocking the way or at least fouling up the path as we try to live a full and meaningful life?

It would be debilitating to live life with your own mortality at the forefront of your mind each day. But don't we owe it to ourselves to think about the shortness of life more often? To take the chance to consider what really matters to us? And then to do everything in our power to live our lives investing in and honoring what we value? With however much time we have? Or in Steve Jobs's words: "Remembering that you are going to die is the best way I know to avoid the trap of thinking you have something to lose. You are already naked. There is no reason not to follow your heart."

TAKE ACTION: Write the answers to the following questions in a journal:

- What is something that I really want in my life and do not have right now?
- What is preventing me from trying to get it?
- What do I currently have in my life that is holding me back—beliefs, objects, relationships, et cetera?
- What am I willing to let go of to obtain or achieve what matters most to me?

CHAPTER 2

The Decluttering Mind-Set

START WITH YOURSELF

Decluttering is a practice in understanding your values and observing how these values are reflected in your physical space. It is essentially a spiritual pursuit. And as with any spiritual undertaking, it is best to start with yourself.

We cannot tell you how many times, when we describe our work to someone new, that person inevitably says, "Oh wow, my (insert family-member title here) *really* needs to hire you." And while that might be true, we always reply, "Sure! As long as your (insert family-member title here) is the one who wants to work with us!"

The plain truth is that you cannot wish (or nag) someone into simplifying a space; when it comes to personal possessions, people don't want to be told what to do or that they have too much. Approaching from this direction makes a person feel defensive and not in control—both of which rarely lead to positive change. A person will only come around to the idea of living a simplified, grounded lifestyle on his or her own terms.

The best way to get anyone else on board—whether this is a spouse, a partner, a roommate, or a child—is to first focus on yourself and relinquish control over the other person's items. Instead,

21

allow them to witness the benefits of minimalism in your life. For Cary, the benefits were packing three times faster than her husband, being done with her portion of the laundry while he was still folding socks, and spending more time reading in bed rather than hunting down an item before sleep. For Kyle, the benefits included avoiding city traffic (and beating her friends to events) by riding her bike, turning taking out her landfill-bound trash into a quarterly chore, and proving that she can still host a lovely dinner with a minimal kitchen setup. All these benefits add up to a happier, more carefree existence that others can't help but notice.

SHARING SPACES

A few years before Cary began practicing minimalism, she and her soon-to-be husband, Cam, moved into an apartment together. They negotiated and bargained and argued about whose duplicate items would stay and whose would have to go. Rather than compromise, they did what any other duo of stubborn twenty-five-year-olds would do: they stuffed two apartments' worth of IKEA dishes and hand-me-downs into one space. The closets were crammed full, and every bit of wall space had furniture against it. But hey, it all fit.

That first night, when Cary bruised her shin on one of the two huge dressers crowding their bedroom, she knew this maximalist life wouldn't work. Although minimalism was not officially on her radar yet, she came to understand that in failing to compromise, she was setting the dangerous precedent of caring more about her stuff than her beloved. She realized that she needed to make a choice—give up some stuff and create a fresh new home with Cam or keep all her stuff and bruise her shins and relationship nightly. It became clear that she needed to let some of her things go, even if it wasn't easy. As the duplicative items left the apartment, the benefits of a more functional and pleasant space became exceedingly clear. What started as Cary compromising and letting go of some furniture eventually evolved into a jointly supported household tenet.

Meanwhile, in another San Francisco neighborhood, Kyle shared a loft with two roommates. The floor plan was unusual (think: box within a box) and natural light was lacking, so she was constantly rearranging the furniture and decor. Kyle's never-ending attempts to overcome the apartment's physical oddities meant the home was a perpetual work in progress. Kyle was exploring (some might say obsessively) to find the best furniture layout to support the primary functions of the space. She would move the sitting area to one side of the room, try it out for a week or two, and then move it again, all the while assuming that her roommates agreed with her every decision.

The raw finishes of the walls beckoned for color experiments, which she answered in the form of a large pink-and-orange mural and oversized art. Several months later, one of Kyle's roommates asked if they could repaint the mural wall into something more neutral. What followed was an open and candid dialogue about the decor of the loft. Kyle learned that while her roommates had stepped aside so she could rearrange to her heart's content, they actually *did* have their own opinions and preferences about the space. And what it came down to was that everyone wanted to participate in the creation of the shared spaces. This was an eye-opening moment for Kyle, as she understood how her passion had steamrolled the process, leaving her roommates feeling that it was easier to act as if they didn't care rather than speak up.

This important lesson has informed New Minimalism's approach to all client design projects. When brainstorming a new direction for a space, we always ensure that all users of the space are present. We encourage everyone to share their opinions when we discuss adding a new piece of furniture, changing the aesthetic, or reconfiguring the furniture layout.

When sharing spaces with others, communication is oh so important. Yes, sometimes it feels as if life has so many moving parts that sitting down to talk about your space can be relegated to pretty much last on your list of things to do. But an open dialogue about your home can be the difference between a happy living situation and an unhappy one. What's even better is that this type of collaboration always leads to the best design solutions. As you start to understand your values and how you want to feel at home, you have to involve your living partners in the most loving and judgment-free way. Because we all deserve to feel represented and taken care of in our homes.

FAMILY LIFE

Both Cary and Kyle were goofy little kids. We each had items we were madly in love with. Kyle had plastic horses of all varieties she set up little worlds for in her room. Cary spent much time before bed each night arranging her dozens of stuffed animals into families so they could all sleep securely—with she herself getting only the smallest corner of the bed. It was a beautiful thing that both of our parents allowed us to be the masters of our own domains. We were able to save up our allowances to buy toys, to play with those toys in our rooms, to outgrow them as kids do. We imagine that if our parents had tightly controlled our spaces, we might have rebelled or resented them and turned into mini-hoarders rather than minimalists!

While some children more than others have a natural proclivity to emotionally attach to and squirrel away objects, there are still methods you can use to work *with* these tendencies. We have observed that even the most sentimental children thrive when they are presented with clear structure and boundaries related to their things. "Too much stuff deprives kids of leisure, and the ability to explore their worlds deeply," says family counselor Kim John Payne. As long as children feel as though they have options and free will within those boundaries, a happy compromise can always be reached. He continues: "We are the adults in our children's lives. . . . We can expand and protect their childhoods by not overloading them with the pseudochoices and the false power of so much *stuff*."

As parents you decide what is purchased and what enters your home, how common areas are shared, and what is stored there. Rather than begin with decluttering your child's room, start instead by modeling the type of behavior you desire by decluttering adult and shared spaces. Have open conversations about why you are donating your unused items and the benefits of doing so. Set up family rules for which items can be stored where. Give your children's toys physical boundaries in order to denote when something is full. Help them learn when the toy bin is too full: when it's overflowing and toys at the bottom are hard to reach. You can then show them how to declutter and donate items, sharing with them the benefits they will experience and the benefits the children in the greater community will receive with those items. There is a delicate balance each family must navigate for itself between establishing firm boundaries and allowing for a child's natural tendencies and desires to be acknowledged. We believe that simply providing your children a clear environment in which they can pretend, imagine, and create will allow them to thrive.

FINDING YOUR "WHY"

When we commence work with a new client, the very first question we ask is "Why?" Why are you choosing to do this? Why is now the right time to take on a complete decluttering project? Why do you think you haven't been able to do this on your own? Why is this so important to you? Here is a sampling of the answers we receive:

"From the moment I walk in the door, I feel overwhelmed. I don't want to feel that way anymore."

———————————

"I don't know how it got so bad, but I'm embarrassed to have people over to my house."

———————————

"I just started yoga and meditation, and I want my home to reflect the peacefulness I'm trying to bring into my life."

———————————

"We are expecting a baby and need to tame our already full home before adding more to it."

———————————

"I recently cleared out my dad's house after he passed away, and I don't want to leave that same mess for anyone else."

While the reasons vary, the common thread among all our clients is that they have undergone some type of transition that has resulted in the realization that time and life are precious.

They don't want to waste any more of that time organizing, looking for, cleaning, rearranging, and managing their stuff. They are ready to spend that time engaged in the activities they enjoy with the people they love.

TAKE ACTION: What is your "why"? Do you want your home to be a sanctuary, a place you associate with rest and rejuvenation? Do you desire an open and flexible furniture layout so that you can easily host a group event? Or do you need your home to be perfectly suited for family life so that everyone's essential items are accounted for and can easily be put away? Having a firm grasp on the reason behind your decluttering effort is the best way to keep your head above water when you are deep into sorting your things. To determine your "why," try the following exercise.

When I walk in the door of my home, I want to feel:

- Relaxed
- Calm
- Inspired
- Creative
- Comfortable
- Healthy

- Clean
- Rejuvenated
- Energized
- Ordered
- Simple
- Lively

- Peaceful
- Grounded
- Balanced
- Proud

Take thirty seconds to write down all the words that intuitively jump out at and motivate you deeply.

Now go back through your selected words and circle the most important three.

Play around with these words—perhaps you want to change *relaxed* to *serene* or maybe even take a moment with a thesaurus to find the exact word that feels right to you.

Write your three selected words on a sticky note, and place it somewhere prominent in the room in which you are decluttering.

A BUYING MORATORIUM

While this process is underway, it is crucial that you refrain from purchasing anything new. Yep, you read that correctly. Except for expendables like food and toilet paper, we are asking you to put a complete halt to your buying. By doing so, the decluttering process will be easier and you will be able to better track your progress. If items continue to enter your home while you declutter, it confuses the process and makes your progress impossible to gauge. What good does it do to bail water from a sinking ship when you haven't plugged the hole yet? And yes, this includes the purchase of any organizational tools, like those cute bins and baskets. The basket you think you need in order to hold item X may very well surface during the decluttering process, or you'll find something basketlike to serve the purpose until you are finished.

Additionally, by agreeing to a strict buying moratorium, you will break the mindless habit of purchasing. You will start to notice the frequency with which you are tempted to buy: when you are in line at the grocery store, during the last twenty-five minutes of an online sale, when you pop into Target for "just that one thing." Like breaking any bad habit, it will not necessarily be easy. But by starting strictly and building self-awareness, you will allow a new habit of intentional purchasing to rise in its place. Your shopping habits will no longer be at the whims of sales or countdown clocks but rather will follow your own personal values. When you regain control over your buying habits, you will feel light, free, and deeply empowered.

NOT LESS FOR THE SAKE OF LESS

The most extreme thing that Cary ever did in her journey to minimalism was to count all of her things. She'd read a book called *The 100 Thing Challenge*. The writer, a gregarious man named Dave Bruno who resided in San Diego, had decided to go all out, living with only a hundred personal items for a year. Impressively, the items that didn't make the list were not stored away in a box somewhere but were donated or sold, a.k.a. gone for good.

Cary happened upon *The 100 Thing Challenge* in the middle of a life-simplification plateau. She'd committed to a simpler life and parted with many belongings but still felt that her home was cluttered. She didn't know the questions to ask or the things to focus on when she hit roadblocks. So, grasping for a solution to this lull, she thought, "Aha! I, too, should own only a hundred things!"

The process of whittling down her stuff to a hundred belongings was much like playing the lo-fi computer game *The Oregon Trail*. She started out fresh and inspired and then quickly felt the grueling process turning on her. Nonetheless, she had a lot of pride on the line. If she had only a hundred things, she believed, she would be enlightened, focused on her creative pursuits, and have such a gloriously vibrant life that people would stop her in the street and say, "You are radiant! What's the secret?" She would then show them a photo of her hundred things on her phone like a proud parent.

Instead, as she got closer to the hundred things goal, the goal itself began to weigh on her. She had to start letting go of objects she used, enjoyed, and loved in order to succeed at the hundred things challenge. She found herself in the same situation she'd been in before she became a minimalist: obsessed with her stuff. But to make matters worse, not only was she always thinking of and dealing with her stuff, she was counting it, too.

Much like a crash diet, when her hundred things challenge was complete, Cary rebounded with a serious consumerist streak. She felt as though she needed to rebel against the restrictive, forced, and unpleasant sensation of not allowing herself to have things that she needed or honestly and deeply desired. There were a dozen or so items she loved that she'd forced herself to part with or told herself she could not purchase during this experiment. So like any yo-yo dieter who leaves a healthy place and enters the land of willpower and restriction, she binged. Cary bought all those things she'd deeply missed and then a whole lot more because she so deeply resented the forced lack of belongings she'd opted into by completing the hundred things challenge.

It took a period of calibrating, having swung wildly from too much to too little, in order to reacquaint herself with the sensation of just right. Months later, when the dust had settled and she felt like herself again, she realized the worthlessness of pursuing less for the sake of less. Just like with food, intense restriction of possessions leads to feelings of anxiety, deprivation, and fear. We know the downfalls of having too much, but it's certainly worth acknowledging the downfalls of having too little.

DECLUTTERING
IS ADDICTIVE

Once you develop the habit of releasing items that don't serve you, you'll wonder how you ever lived with so much stuff; it feels amazing. Much like the endorphin rush you receive from exercise, you'll crave the feeling of a calm, decluttered house. However, in order to tap into this wellspring of good feelings and ease, you first have to see the light of day. You have to feel the ease with which you are able to go about your day-to-day life; you have to experience firsthand the lightness and satisfaction that come with a simpler lifestyle. Doing so will likely require that you cross the line of your personal comfort level to venture into "too few" territory. As long as it is not life threatening, testing out the smallest number of items you can live with in a particular category is all part of the process. Kyle, for example, lives in a studio apartment with only six glasses. These glasses are used for everything from water to smoothies to fancy wine to unfancy wine. On the rare occasion that she hosts more than six people at a time, she either borrows glasses from a friend (e.g., a planned party) or her guests drink out of mugs (e.g., an unplanned party). And the most magical thing about it is that, either way, everyone seems to have a great time. Similar to a juice cleanse, decluttering is about resetting, perhaps experiencing the slight scarcity that we are programmed to be afraid of, and then finding balance again.

CHAPTER 3

The Archetypes

UNCOVERING YOUR
EMOTIONAL STYLE
OF RELATING TO
YOUR POSSESSIONS

We've had the privilege of working with a diverse group of clients, from Silicon Valley executives who hop on a private plane to attend a meeting as soon as our session is finished, to recent college graduates renting a humble bedroom in a shared apartment, to couples making room for their first or second child, to the recently divorced.

Since our top aim is to tailor each space to the inhabitant's unique needs, we have to learn a lot about our clients, and fast. We do this the old-fashioned way: by asking literally hundreds of questions. What are your big goals for the space? What are your big goals in life? What is your aesthetic? How often do you use this item? What about this item that seems so similar to the others you kept? Why do you think this part of your home simply isn't working?

After thousands of hours getting to know people and their stuff, we noticed several distinct categories and patterns of behaviors across seemingly different populations. Thus, the archetypes emerged, naturally, over countless lunch breaks and hours spent traveling to and from sessions, discussing our sessions, as a way to describe how people relate to their possessions. Basically, it came down to answering the questions, *why* is decluttering hard for this particular person and *how* can we communicate with them most effectively?

In time, we became exceptionally attuned to the nuances in language as well as a host of nonverbal cues (which often speak volumes). After all, we are meeting people in the most vulnerable places of their homes—the chaos under the bed, the closet where everything gets shoved before guests come over, the piles of unopened mail overflowing in a hidden drawer. We quickly learned that when vulnerability is high, defenses are, too. The key to keeping communication open is to meet people exactly where they're at. Some people need numbers, percentages, and citations from recent efficiency studies, whereas statistics can shut others down.

Eventually we teased apart four archetypes so that we could use them as a type of shorthand in communicating with one another throughout our client sessions. Cary could simply say to a client, "I can tell how important your relationships are to you," and Kyle would instantly know how to best communicate with the client and what to prioritize in her designs. And the most fascinating part? These archetypes, or patterns of behavior, didn't seem in any way to be connected to external factors: wealth, living situation, marital status, et cetera.

Once we understand a client's mental space and values, we know what to say and how to say it when he or she hits a block. Over time, we became experts in the communication style of each archetype, and thus could effectively speak with clients using rationale and motivation to suit their needs, rather than attempt to communicate the same point in endless different ways. In this chapter, we are handing you the keys to cultivating self-awareness of your own archetype so that you can get the most out of your decluttering work.

HOW TO USE
THIS CHAPTER

In the following sections, we describe each archetype in depth. At the end of each section is a series of questions for you to answer thoughtfully yet rapidly, tapping into the subconscious lens through which you view the world. Note: the harder you think each question through, the less likely you are to tap into your primal gut reaction. Keep track of all your answers in a journal.

Take note of any specific situations you recall when asking yourself these questions.

Don't judge yourself or hold on too hard to specific words or ideas you use, but do your best to be as honest as possible. Feeling stuck? It can be helpful to elicit the opinions of those with whom you have a close relationship to help you determine what archetype best reflects your tendencies. Your close friends and family might be able to offer some wisdom through their objectivity.

If you answer yes to the majority of the questions in each section, you will know that you strongly identify with that archetype. You may find that you identify with more than one. Your archetypes are not labels you are burdened to carry with you for the rest of your days; they're simply powerful self-awareness tools to make this act of decluttering simpler, more meaningful, and longer lasting.

THE FOUR ARCHETYPES

We've defined four distinct archetypes, each named for the way in which it is positively expressed: Connected, Practical, Energetic, and Frugal. These archetypes are not mutually exclusive; rather, they are states of being. You may find that a certain archetype resonates more with you depending on the particular *category of things* you are addressing in your home. For example, dealing with memorabilia inherently calls up the Connected (emotional) archetype. Dealing with technology almost always taps into the Practical (logical) archetype. Still, you will likely find that you default to one particular archetype 95 percent of the time. For example, consider your personality at work versus at home. Each physical domain might call for you to accentuate a certain area of your personality. Nonetheless, the dominant aspects of your disposition remain across all interactions. The greatest value in uncovering your archetype is that we're going to give you the tools to coach yourself—with compassion and empathy and a little tough love—to let go of the items that no longer serve you.

THE SHADOW SIDE   Each archetype is inherently full of strengths, which shine most clearly when we're in a state of trust, openness, and presence. Each archetype also possesses a "shadow side" that convinces you to keep things you don't really want or need in your life. It is the flip side of the same coin—the same modality but with a different manifestation.

Each shadow side is unique to the particular archetype, yet they all emerge under the same conditions: when we are feeling fear or mistrust, or when we are focused on what happened in the past or attached to a hypothetical future. To be clear, the shadow side usually arises due to internal emotions, not outside circumstances. We've had a client in the middle of nearly debilitating chemotherapy treatments be deeply present, open, and trusting. She was calm and positive throughout the decluttering process, even though no one would blame her for feeling anything but that.

We've also observed clients who possess massive wealth and superb health and are surrounded by positive relationships who are painfully stuck in the shadow side of their archetype. While their circumstances are seemingly perfect, their minds are rooted in past experiences of struggle or mistrust or anchored by fear of a conjured future.

In this shadow state, decluttering, in any meaningful sense, is nearly impossible; you simply cannot be clear on what is actually most important to you in your life. All kinds of fear-based reasons emerge: "I might need that" or "This cost a lot" or "One day I'll have the time to finish that project." You cannot create a calming, inspired home from a place of fear. You cannot bless and release things that are weighing you down and holding you back when life feels untrustworthy.

The first step is awareness. Once you know your primary archetype, it will be far easier to catch yourself entering the shadow side. The second step is to consciously return to your core self, the positive manifestation of the archetype. We are not asking you to change your archetype; we are simply asking you to activate its positive aspects.

ARCHETYPE #1: CONNECTED

SHADOW SIDE: Clinging

BLOCK: Sentimentality

HAS A HARD TIME LETTING GO OF: Gifts, handwritten cards, travel souvenirs, ticket stubs

The Connected archetype has an emotional, relational, and impassioned way of approaching the world. These people treasure family, friendships, and partnerships above all else. They love to make those they care about feel good. Connected types tend to be wonderful hosts, the people you can rely on to throw a great party, send you a birthday card, or remember that important date on the calendar.

Connected types dwell in the present; they are focused on whoever is in front of them in the moment. They are exceptional listeners who try their best to offer thoughtful and compassionate advice. Connected types act from a place of interrelatedness, bestowing a reverence upon the people and things in their lives.

The Shadow Side of Connected: Clinging

———

Clinging's motto: "But that was a gift" or "That was from a trip" or "That reminds me of someone important."

"Oh no, I have to keep those!" Kate said, with a panicked look at the box of plastic baby rattles Cary held.

"Why is that?" Cary asked gently.

"Because it's from my friend's baby shower. I hosted the party and had these custom made for all the guests. I have to keep those."

Kate took the box from Cary's hands and quickly tucked it away, out of Cary's reach and view, and moved on to the next item to sort.

Our client Kate had saved every birthday, thank-you, and holiday card she'd received in the past ten years. She had bins and boxes full of ticket stubs from every event she'd attended, along with menus, place cards, and other miscellaneous tokens from each event, including photos of her and the guests who'd attended the event with her. The entirety of her wedding decorations occupied a large portion of her basement room. She had a closet filled with blank cards and gifts saved so that at any moment she would have something to give to one of her friends or family members. Yet when those special events came around, she inevitably purchased a new card or gift to perfectly match the occasion or giftee. In short, Kate's home had turned into one big box of rattles: things she didn't use, enjoy, or display yet was terrified of letting go. Why?

Kate was acting from the shadow side of the Connected archetype: Clinging. She was a treasured friend, a beloved wife and mother, and a high-powered manager at work, and she was often surrounded by people who loved and respected her, but she never felt as though her actions were enough. She felt she needed to hold on to every little physical thing that was associated with these events, these people, and her past experiences. *I have to* and *I should* were common phrases in her vocabulary. She pushed herself to near exhaustion and deep frustration trying to memorialize every event in her life.

After several sessions of working together to declutter the overwhelming number of sentimental items in her home, we learned that Kate's natural tendency toward connecting with her friends and family had been deeply compromised in the past. Kate had experienced an extremely challenging childhood, one where she did not feel taken care of or special in any way. She never wanted anyone in her life to experience this same deficiency, so she was making up for it by being the very best friend, mom, wife, and aunt she possibly could be.

A big part of the Clinging experience is that of being caught in the past. Kate's fear was palpable as she considered parting with plastic rattles that she hadn't seen in years, had never used, and never would. This fear- and anxiety-based sensation veiled all her decisions. As a result, she was surrounded by her past, and that past was preventing her from clearing a bold path forward.

Connected people will venture toward the shadow side of their emotional style when they confuse the physical object with the actual relationship or experience itself. They feel that if they give up the objects related to a relationship, they are devaluing the relationship; they're afraid they will lose important people or memories if they don't hold on to all the evidence.

Once Kate was able to recognize how her past trauma related to her current habitual behavior, she began to regain control over her decision making. She was able to see how *she*, not her stuff, was the active agent in her experience in her home. Slowly she began to trust that she could simply keep the emotional memories of the events without having to keep all the physical mementos.

Block: Sentimentality

The main thing blocking Connected types from releasing items is sentimentality. If an object is in any way linked to a relationship—such as a gift or a note, or a photograph or a souvenir from a shared experience—Clinging people will hold on to it even if they do not use or enjoy it.

Ask yourself

If you answer yes to more than half of these questions, you exhibit Clinging tendencies.

— Do you value your close relationships above all else?
— If you were stranded on a desert island, would you bring companions over objects?
— Do you consider yourself to have a strong emotional attachment to more than half of the items in your home?
— Do more than half of the items in your home remind you of a particular person, a place you traveled to, or an event you attended?
— Do you feel as though you need to keep every piece of memorabilia associated with a positive experience in order to honor the experience and retain the memory?
— Do you commemorate experiences from other people's lives?

— Does it feel sad, scary, or disrespectful to let go of something that was given to you as a gift, regardless of whether you use or enjoy it?

— When you put on an item of clothing, do you often remember who you were with or where you were when you purchased it?

Tool for Moving from
Clinging Back to Connected

First, remember that your memories and experiences are separate from your possessions. We like to use the phrase "Collect memories, not things" to sum up the idea that it's not actually the objects we love but the memories they reference. Start by first freeing yourself of the obligation to memorialize every event from your past with a physical memento. Trust that you will naturally recall specific memories or experiences as you continue to live out your days.

When deciding to part with an item of sentimental value, take a moment to "bless and release" it. Rather than dumping a broken travel token in the trash or throwing a gifted sweater in the donation bin, give yourself a moment to honor the item. Appreciate it and the person or circumstance that brought it into your life. Hug the item (or smell it or pat it) one last time, and say aloud an expression of gratitude, like "Thank you, ugly Christmas sweater. You came into my life as such a thoughtful gift, and I release you to keep someone else warm and happy this winter."

ARCHETYPE #2: PRACTICAL

The Shadow Side of Practical: Limited

Limited's motto: "I could probably use that to _____."

SHADOW SIDE: Limited

BLOCK: Usefulness

HAS A HARD TIME LETTING GO OF: Art supplies, craft supplies, electrical cords, old nails and screws, scrap materials

The Practical archetype operates from the logical hub of the mind. It is a data-driven, methodical, and factual way of approaching the world. The Practical archetype comes into play when there is a task at hand, an actionable item, an objective to be met, or a question that needs to be answered. These people are often engineering wizards: deductive, strategic, and pragmatic. They creatively find ways to improve a scenario, figure out the most efficient route to a destination, or make extra space in a dishwasher that is already full. This archetype always reminds us of our childhood hero, MacGyver.

When operating from the shadow side, Practical types are Limited, unaware of the latent effect their things have on them. They are unaware of or able to ignore how a cluttered space negatively impacts them and, more often, how their space affects other people. They can often be rigid in their opinions, seeing only one truth according to the data at hand. Though it may be practical to hold on to things that might be useful in a hypothetical future, it ends up limiting space for their *present day* needs and life.

Limited types also have a narrow understanding of *use*; they consider only the absolute usefulness of an item, not taking into account an item's actual usefulness to them in their present lives. They can easily compartmentalize their chaotic, disordered homes to lead otherwise highly functioning, orderly lives. Take, for example, our client Shawn. When Shawn first contacted us, he was unemotional when talking about his space. He never indicated that he was frustrated or overwhelmed—he seemed nonchalant about the disorder of his home, the chaos of which had driven him to occasionally book a hotel room rather than sleep in his own bedroom. In addition, he had begun to suffer from severe allergies and sleep apnea due to the buildup of dust and clutter throughout his room.

Shawn was a highly in-demand Silicon Valley engineer—a man who was flown around the country to attend conferences—and his time was so valuable that it didn't seem worth it to him to deal with his stuff. He eventually came to acknowledge that the chaos was negatively impacting his ability to get to work on time, to find items, and to pack for trips, which was when he decided to work with us.

He kept the bulk of his clutter—electronic components, travel-sized toiletries, free T-shirts and other swag from conferences and events—around because he knew these things were inherently useful. He could always build a new system from his boxes of electronic components—*I might have a lot of free time and decide that would be a fun project someday!* he reasoned. Or, *At some point, I might want to refer to those engineering textbooks and articles from college—they had useful information in them!* As a frequent traveler, he maintained that he would eventually need all twenty travel-sized tubes of toothpaste. While all these reasons seem valid, they are concurrently the cause of all the clutter and the barrier to a simplified home.

Over four sessions, we helped Shawn complete a deep, sweeping purge of all the items that had accumulated in his bedroom, a room that also served as his home office and personal living room. As our work progressed, we learned that despite his overflowing space, he was able to travel for weeks at a time with just a backpack's worth of things. He was also an early adopter of the "work uniform," wearing nearly the same outfit each day. He truly *was* a minimalist at heart. He had just formed a Limited way of dealing with the abundance of small, semiuseful items that came into his life, because he could not see beyond their usefulness to the ways in which they were hindering him.

We watched Shawn come to terms with the fact that just because an item was useful in theory did not mean it was useful to *him*. Instead, all these "useful" items were making it nearly impossible for him to access the things he needed each day. Removing the accumulation of clutter allowed him to navigate the rest of his life without an underlying sense of chaos. When he finally experienced how grounded and calm his space felt without the extra stuff, he was able to see how it had been negatively affecting him. His newfound clarity even helped him realize that he was ready for a real change, and he decided to move to Los Angeles! Without drawing the connection between his clutter and his subconscious feelings of chaos and being overwhelmed, who knows how long it would have taken for Shawn to move into this next exciting chapter.

Block: Usefulness

The central idea blocking Limited types from releasing items is usefulness. If an object has a perceived use—for any person in any circumstance—practical people will hold on to it even if it is not useful to them.

Ask yourself

If you answer yes to more than half of these questions, you exhibit Limited tendencies.

— Are people often impressed by your ability to bootstrap or come up with creative solutions?
— Are you the go-to person for technical or strategic problems?
— Do you find it hard to get rid of items that are in some way or another "useful"?
— Do you conjure elaborate hypothetical future scenarios in which you might need a certain item?

_ Do you keep a variety of cords, plugs, and chargers around, even if you don't know what they go to?

_ Do you strongly identify with your ability to make do and find creative solutions to use what you already have instead of buying something new?

_ Do you feel that an object's usefulness is more important than anything else?

_ Do you like to collect bits of information, in the form of magazines, clipped articles, newspapers, et cetera, in case you might want to refer back to them someday?

Tool for Moving from Limited Back to Practical

When you're operating from the Limited mind-set, you'll notice that any and all "useful" items get a free pass to stay in your home. The problem here is that there are millions of things in the world that have utility, and if you want a clutter-free home, you're going to have to drastically increase your standards for what is allowed to stay. The key here is to remove hypothetical situations from your reasoning to keep an item. Notice if you start with phrases like "I might" or "I could" when thinking about an item. Instead, focus on the present moment and your current needs. Even if an item is in theory useful, do *you* need it *right now*? If not, err on the side of donating it—someone else will certainly use and enjoy it.

Before decluttering, it is helpful for Practical types to identify organizations that are willing and able to accept their donations of useful items so that they won't be discarded. In the Resources section we have a number of suggestions for how you can find local organizations that would love to accept your donations.

LETTING GO OF "JUST IN CASE"

Do you want to know the most common pain point that shows up in a decluttering session? The idea of keeping something "just in case." Often it shows up in response to our suggestion that clients might prefer to donate an item they've never used, don't particularly like, or wish they'd never purchased to begin with. (Think: a third box of extra staples in a paperless office, a dress two sizes too small with the tags still on, a stack of old and unread magazines that might contain an article that they might want to refer to if they do decide to learn to sew, after all.) With incredulous stares, clients ask us, "But what if I need it someday?" or "Shouldn't I keep it, you know, just in case?"

First and foremost, yes, it is entirely possible that, one day, you might need this thing in question. It would be pointless for us to debate otherwise. And yet, if that day comes and you do in fact need this thing that you now don't have—what will happen? How hard will it be to replace, or make do with something else? Withstanding the possibility of needing this thing in the future is part of moving from the shadow side to the positive side of your archetype.

Here are three reasons to let go of "just in case" items:

1 **Consider the costs of keeping the item.** Humans have evolved to be more motivated to avoid pain than to seek joy. Meaning that as a species we're naturally going to give more weight to the fear of having to potentially reacquire something than the pleasure of an uncluttered space. What our limbic (lizard) brain is not considering, however, is the less obvious pain of keeping so much stuff around. We don't consider what a burden it is to maintain these items. We don't consider all the physical space and mental energy they take up. We forget about the hard, crappy decisions we have to make (like spending a gorgeous weekend cleaning

up the garage or deciding against moving to a new home we love because there isn't enough storage), all in service of these items that *we don't even use*.

2 **Experience the joy of knowing what you *don't* have.** Imagine you need to find your third-favorite, less-than-perfect raincoat that you've kept "just in case." You might first look in your closet. Then the coat closet. Then in the attic where you store your winter gear. Then perhaps in your camping bin. Or maybe it's with your costumes under the bed? Or is it possible that you lent it to a friend a while back? Forty-five minutes later, you're sweaty, frustrated, and still don't know where the raincoat is.

Instead, if you adopt the habit of releasing extra just-in-case items, you'll know right away *what* you have and *where* it is—and you'll also know what you *don't* have. Rather than waste time searching or retracing your thought process, you can jump right into borrowing, substituting, or making do without. Trust us, this under-acknowledged benefit is supremely liberating.

3 **Leave space for yourself to grow.** Whenever we hold on to items "just in case," we're locking our future selves into a certain way of being. One of the most beautiful things about being human is that we are constantly evolving as people. Our habits, priorities, and hobbies shift and vary as we navigate this wild life. When you hold on to old items "just in case," you're committing to staying in place—to having those same exact interests or living in the same space. When you let go of those items, you are giving yourself permission to be flexible, to grow and change.

ARCHETYPE #3: ENERGETIC

SHADOW SIDE: Scattered

BLOCK: Saying no

HAS A HARD TIME LETTING GO OF: Projects, personal and social commitments

People who operate primarily in the Energetic archetype joyfully move through the world at a pace and with an efficacy that make those around them stare in wonder. The Energetic archetype is a physical way of approaching the world; it radiates energy throughout the body, into the limbs. These people have great stores of energy and zeal, which they use to tackle any project or obstacle in their way. They tend to be innovators at work or deeply committed to their hobbies. They're often do-it-yourselfers, or folks who love projects, learning something new, or trying something different.

The Shadow Side of Energetic: Scattered

Scattered's motto: "I can do it all."

The shadow side of the Energetic archetype is that same, vibrant energy but refracted through a crystal. These people are, in one word, Scattered. Despite being passionate and engaging, this type often starts but rarely finishes projects. They say yes to most things, are chronic over-schedulers, and typically run ten minutes late to everything. Their spaces are filled with aspirational to-dos and projects in progress. They often experience guilt as a result of not completing their projects yet cannot maintain focus long enough to complete something before moving on to the next. It's common for our clients who display this type of behavior to cite being diagnosed with ADD or ADHD.

Take, for example, our lovely client Mei. When we started working with Mei, we were amazed by all that she accomplished every day. A powerhouse attorney with a successful practice,

Mei was also a beloved wife and a mother to two precious young children. Prior to family life, Mei was known as a go-getter at her firm. She was always the one who could step up to the plate, take more on, say yes to anything. She spent her already minimal free time trying out new types of exercise, cooking new cuisines, and learning new crafts.

With the added commitment of spending quality time with her young family, Mei now felt overwhelmed. All the things at work and at home that called for her time and attention felt oppressive and boundless. She felt as though she could never just sit down quietly with a book or get into bed early with her husband because piled around her were her mounting to-dos. Mei surmised that putting into place a number of complicated systems and infrastructure for all her projects would be key to helping her feel calm at home.

We met her several weeks after her youngest child's birthday party at their family home. It felt as if the party had just ended, with Mei's handmade decorations, letterpress invitations, and elaborate goody bags still scattered throughout the house. She was too tired to clean up, she told us, after staying up late for several nights preparing for the party. As we toured her home, we noticed piles of half-completed projects in nearly every room. Mei said her husband loved her creativity but felt burdened by her best-laid plans never being completed and instead constantly filling up their space.

Throughout our several sessions together, we helped Mei see that as a working parent, her time was already almost 100 percent spoken for. Her free time was very limited and therefore should be treated as the precious commodity that it was. Rather than create elaborate systems to hold projects she would never have the time to finish, we encouraged her to be realistic with the time she had and prioritize what was most important.

Eventually, Mei was able to let go of every extra project that was in process in her home. She committed to taking on no more than one manageable extracurricular project at any time, helping her maintain a sense of peace and calm at home, which then radiated out to her sense of calm at work. We designated space in a specific cabinet to hold her one in-process project, noting that if the cabinet was full, the project needed to be either completed or released before she could take on something new. She was amazed by how intuitive and simple the new system was and how liberating it felt to walk into her home and not have anything to do other than enjoy her family.

Block: Saying no

The central idea blocking Scattered types is the idea of saying no to things. Because they love to try new hobbies, start new projects, and learn something different, they have a hard time prioritizing because they want to do everything.

Ask yourself

If you answer yes to more than half of these questions, you exhibit Scattered tendencies.

— Do you have a number of hobbies or activities you are passionate about?
— Are you known as a Jack- or Jill-of-all-trades?
— Do others often compliment you on your vibrant energy?
— Is your to-do list long and unwieldy, some might say unrealistic?
— Do you find it hard to say no to commitments of your time and energy, even when you know that you are being stretched too thin?
— Do you find yourself often running five to ten minutes late?
— Do you often underestimate the amount of time a project will take, forcing you to leave it incomplete as you move on to other obligations?
— When you find yourself with free time, do you feel burdened by the need to wrap up a number of things you've already begun?

Tool for Moving from
Scattered Back to Energetic

You suffer from wanting to do it all, so you likely have many aspirational, unfinished projects around the house. Any project that is incomplete is telling you something: either it is not a priority or you are being unrealistic with your time. Releasing the objects related to these projects not only honors the objects themselves so that they can be used and appreciated by someone else but also gives you a second chance—a chance to start anew and decide how you would like to spend your time now that you're no longer filled with a sense of duty to complete all these half-started projects. It requires self-forgiveness, for sure. But let us remind you that you can still be a good friend, even if you don't knit that scarf.

For scheduling, mentally step back and consider your top priorities in your work and personal life. This could be anything from quality time with family to training for a triathlon to earning that promotion at work. Write the top three down. Now look at your actual calendar of upcoming events and projects; does the way you spend your time match what you value most? If you see discrepancies, practice saying no to any activity that doesn't align with how you've just stated you would like to spend your time. Moving forward, actually schedule time for the activities and actions that support your top priorities. Even if it's just a phone call to your best friend, formally setting aside your time will ensure that it doesn't get filled with something less important that might crop up the day of.

To-do lists are your best friends. Take the time to find the system that works best for you. Kyle has her notebook, which follows her to and from work, which she liberally writes to-do lists in. She then ruthlessly tears the lists out at the end of each day. Anything that is super important but wasn't finished gets transferred to the next day. Practice writing a to-do list each morning or the beginning of the week. This will help you pause to think about the essentials you need to make space for. Everything else is optional, just icing on the cake.

ARCHETYPE #4: FRUGAL

BLOCK: Money

HAS A HARD TIME LETTING GO OF: Anything with monetary worth or perceived rarity

The Shadow Side of Frugal: Scarcity

Scarcity's motto:
"I might never be able to replace this."

People who operate from the Frugal archetype tend to act from a place of mindful self-awareness and contentment. They plan for the future but are rooted in the present moment, viewing their surroundings with clarity. Frugal types have thoughtfully uncovered their most important goals and choose to spend their resources in ways that are aligned with those highest priorities. They thoughtfully eliminate expenses that do not add to their health, joy, or goals for happiness. They prioritize what is most important and use their resources to highlight these priorities. People who operate in the Frugal state are centered and intentional with how they expend their energy.

In the shadow side of Frugal lies Scarcity. Scarcity has little to do with a person's current state of wealth, because Scarcity dwells in replaying problems from the past or projecting anxieties into the future. People operating from a place of Scarcity feel unstable, ill at ease, and unsure, and they hold on to the items around them in an attempt to quell these fears. They typically rely on outside circumstances to soothe their internal discomfort. This reactionary behavior often stems from some trauma experienced in the past.

When we met our client Mark, he was in a constant state of Scarcity. He desired a calming oasis and knew the stuff around him was constantly distracting him and keeping him busy. In his life, he had experienced several turns of excellent luck. He'd scored a great job and an incredible deal on a lovely house and now had a surplus of cash with which he was treating himself to our service. Yet even in this state of objective wealth, Mark simply could not let go of old items for fear that someday he would need them and he wouldn't be able to afford them. He held on to out-of-date medication (like, *decades* old), reused old paper napkins, and wouldn't allow himself the luxury of buying some of the things he needed (like a new pair of formal shoes). He held on to receipts for years and had dozens of old, very inexpensive items he hoped to return for pennies on the dollar.

After we decluttered his clothing and toiletries, we got down to the piles of paperwork and receipts that had been cluttering the house. Mark eventually shared with us that as a child, his family had experienced an extended period of poverty. They barely had the essentials and continually had to make compromises to satisfy their basic needs. This feeling of scarcity and this fear that things might not work out were continuing to taint Mark's current-day experience, over forty years later. Even after he earned his doctorate and had a long, successful teaching career, his relationship with his possessions was shrouded in this darkness. It took sitting down to sort old receipts and crumpled napkins to make this connection. We find that when our clients are willing to do the work, to sit down and face all the reasons they allow the clutter to accumulate, they have the biggest breakthroughs.

Block: Money

The central idea blocking Scarcity types from releasing items is money. They hold tight to any object that they spent money on, whether expensive or perceived to have high worth, regardless of whether that object is useful or pleasurable.

— Are you deeply intentional about how you choose to spend your money?

— Do you have a budget in place for your expenses?

— Do you frequently check your bank accounts or credit card bills?

— Do you tend to plan and save up for a while for special items or trips that are very important to you?

— Do you hold on to things you don't need because you worry you won't be able to afford to repurchase them in the future?

— Do you save receipts, even for minor purchases, in case something happens to an item?

— Do you feel guilty if you don't use up every last bit of an item?

— Do you tend to save and put off using valuable items for future use, often causing them to go bad or become obsolete before you ever find the time to use them?

Tool for Moving from Scarcity Back to Frugal

Come up with a list of at least three practices that have worked in the past to calm and center you in situations of stress.

Examples include:

- Going for a walk
- Sitting in nature
- Dancing to a favorite song
- Journaling
- Breaking a sweat
- Taking twenty device-free minutes to savor a cup of coffee or tea
- Calling up a loved one

List these practices in your journal, and plan to utilize them if you're having trouble with a particular category down the road.

CHAPTER 4

Decluttering + Design

Decluttering and design go hand in hand. We've found that your decluttered home won't feel complete without also reworking the design of your space. For example, once you declutter, you may find that you've created more space in your hall closet, allowing your linens to be stored there instead of in your bedroom. You may eliminate the need for entire pieces of furniture altogether, allowing you to open up the flow of a room with a new furniture arrangement. There may be the opportunity to repurpose items that you already own. This list of possibilities is only limited by your imagination.

During one of our sessions working with a lovely family in San Francisco, we were evaluating the master bedroom and came to the conclusion that a white IKEA bedside table was no longer relevant for the design of the space. Our clients were ready to invest in bedside tables that matched the quality and style of the rest of their bedroom furniture. Later in the day, as we were redesigning the master closet, we saw the need for a shoe rack. Instead of discarding the old IKEA bedside table and advising our clients to buy a shoe rack, we turned the table on its side, removed a shelf, and bam! Instant shoe rack. What's even better is that this repurposed former bedside table was actually sturdier and more functional than any shoe rack we would have found in the store.

At the other end of the spectrum, it is possible that as you finish decluttering your home it will be obvious that you are in need of a key piece of furniture or organizational infrastructure. The benefit of having decluttered *before* purchasing any items is that you'll be able to buy precisely what you need. Buying one or two pivotal pieces to complete a decluttered room is far kinder to your wallet and the environment than completely redecorating a room that wasn't working in the first place because it was simply overcrowded.

ENVISIONING YOUR NEW SPACE

Even before delving into your decluttering efforts, it is important to envision how you would like to use your space in all its newly decluttered glory. This process is very much like finding your "why," as we detailed in Chapter 2, but with design and function in mind.

TAKE ACTION: Often when we first move into a home, we place furniture where we think it will work best but imagine we will perhaps move it at a later date if it's not the best fit. We cannot tell you how many clients, when asked about the specifics of a less-than-ideal furniture arrangement, say, "That's just where the movers put it when we moved in."

This is your chance for a fresh start. Try to pretend you are in a stranger's home. When looking at your space objectively, do you see furniture that fails in more ways than it satisfies? Is there a furniture arrangement that could better facilitate the primary functions of your space?

Ask yourself these questions to get started:

What is the number-one activity that will take place in each room? Is it a place to entertain guests or a place to recenter and rejuvenate? Whatever your selected primary activity is, the redesign of your space should support this first and foremost.

Next, consider the bones of your specific space, the fixed elements. Step back and assess. What architectural elements would you like to highlight and what would you like to hide? Maybe you have some oddly placed heating vents that you can camouflage with paint. Or perhaps you have some unfortunately colored floor tiles that you can draw less attention to with an area rug.

Try to look at your space as if you were just moving in but with the added benefit of knowing exactly how you use and engage with the space. Do you find that when working from home you gravitate toward the areas with the best natural light? Is it too drafty to sit near the windows during winter? Where would you place the furniture armed with this insider information? As a bonus, the more you declutter, the easier it is to move bookcases and couches (there is less stuff in the way). So try a few different furniture layouts, involve your family/roommates, and play.

SQUARE FOOTAGE:
A REALITY CHECK

A good chunk of our process is devoted to helping clients come to terms with the physical limitations of their space. A cluttered home is often indicative of simply asking too much of the space. How can one small extra bedroom function as your guest room, exercise room, home office, *and* storage space for seasonal clothing? How can your entryway closet contain your everyday bags and jackets when it is bursting with skis and sports gear?

If your home is small, as many of our urban clients' homes are, it's crucial to know what your priorities are and to design your space accordingly. Because while it is possible to have the above-mentioned small bedroom fulfill all those functions, there needs to be a hierarchy, a focus, a priority. If you work from home every day, your space should be optimized for all your home office needs. If, and only if, extra square footage remains once that primary need is satisfied, then you can consider whether an air mattress, a TRX suspension trainer, or your winter gear will also fit without sacrificing your home-office priorities.

If you happen to live in a larger home, a different lens is required. Above all else, do not rush to fill up a large home. It's OK, lovely and liberating even, for extraneous rooms to be simply furnished. Let a child's playroom be an open space for creativity instead of filling it with stations and bins and hundreds of toys. If you are fortunate enough to have a guest room, place just a bed, a bedside table, and perhaps a small dresser inside. Do not—please, please do not—allow your wardrobe to flow into the guest closet. Inevitably this clothing will go unworn, managing your wardrobe will require even more effort, and your guests will feel strange attempting to store their clothing alongside your fancy cocktail dresses. A simple room and an open closet will allow your guests to feel right at home (it will also make preparing for their arrival a breeze). This goes for any extra closet, room, or storage area. Just because you have the space does not mean you have to fill it. And when it comes time to move or downsize, you will be so grateful you've stayed lean while living large.

SYSTEMS: THE GOOD, THE BAD, AND THE TOTALLY EXCESSIVE

Many of our clients, when discussing their goals for their homes, say, "If I just had a system for _____ (dealing with the kids' artwork, putting away laundry, storing all my shoes), it would work." These are the people who either have a hard time developing systems in the first place or who are convinced that the "right" system will solve their clutter problems. The latter group loves elaborate color-coded binders filled with alphabetized tabs, complex filing systems, and specialized calendaring techniques for every segment of their lives.

While basic systems are necessary and create order in a chaotic world, it's those complicated, time-consuming systems that add another layer of to-dos to your already overstrained life. The time required to maintain these systems inevitably proves to be too much. With a considerable up-front investment of time, those well-intended systems are implemented and attended to once or twice, but then they eventually fall into disarray. How do we know this? The proof is in the disorganized pudding. When you look around your home, can you identify some systems that you've implemented yet are not being maintained? Those unkept systems are your evidence that they require too much of your time to maintain and are not actually making your life easier.

Follow these guidelines when creating your own systems within the home:

- **Keep it simple.** Any system that requires multiple complicated steps will likely experience a breakdown. We prefer systems that can be maintained with a single hand—like dropping your keys and wallet into a dish right by the door.
- **Keep like with like.** Splicing categories or having multiple homes for the same items quickly snowballs into confusion and chaos. Instead, keep all items related to the same subcategory in the same place. While this may not apply to a subcategory like pens and pencils in a three-story home, it does apply to how you store your camping gear.
- **Refrain from overly categorizing.** For example, don't worry about wool versus cotton, three-quarter versus full-length sleeves, or V-neck versus scoop neck. Simply group all six of your sweaters in one place.
- **Be realistic and work with your natural tendencies.** If you prefer to cook at home, you probably don't need a dedicated file for take-out food options.
- **Acknowledge that a habit shift might actually be all you need.** For example, putting your reusable shopping bags back in the car after you unload your groceries.

Take the time to find the systems that work for you, and then stick to them! If you went through the trouble to install hooks in the entryway to hang your jackets, yet the jackets always end up on the couch, what is the problem? Is it that the hooks are always full of bags? Is it that you and your partner haven't agreed to this new way of doing things? Are the hooks placed too high for your children to easily access them on their own? Or do you need to change your own habits?

While we recommend systems that are easy to maintain and require little effort, it's important to note that they never require *no* effort. Sometimes it is helpful to create little reminders or incentives for yourself to ensure that systems are completed.

For instance, Kyle came to utilize what she calls the "jacket rule." When she first comes home, she removes her shoes but keeps her jacket on until she has put away everything that has just entered the house. Only after she has unloaded her groceries, opened and sorted the mail, and removed her notebook and laptop from her bag is she allowed to remove her jacket, signifying that she has finished entering the house. Bonus: once you have a simpler lifestyle, you'll notice that you bring fewer and fewer things into your home. Groceries are the only things that enter our households with any regularity.

Of course, implementing systems can get a little trickier when there are multiple people involved. Be it family life or roommate life, the key to any household-wide system is that it needs to be fully agreed upon by all members. When in doubt, overcommunicate to ensure everyone agrees with expectations. For example, if shoes are scattered throughout the house rather than stowed in the front hall, it might not be entirely clear that you are striving for a shoes-free household. Maybe the constant bags in the living room are due to that one roommate who doesn't know the decree to keep the common spaces clear of personal effects. Whatever the intended system, if you get pushback from others, it's time to sit down and be solution oriented. How can you work together to develop a system that works for everyone?

FIVE PLACES ORGANIZATION GOES TO DIE

Below are five common organizational techniques that tend to fail. These are the black holes of organization—the places that unwanted and unneeded items go to collect dust and take up physical and mental space until we make the decision to let them go.

- **Under-the-bed bins.** Though typically purchased to make a person's possessions fit within the ten-by-ten-foot cells known as college dorm rooms, these terrible items sometimes make their way into the adult homes of many of our clients. Not only does keeping rarely used items in plastic limit breathability, making them smell bad, but these items are often completely forgotten about once hidden under the bed. These bins also make it far more difficult to clean beneath your bed, contributing to dust bunnies and allergies. Also worth noting: storing anything under the bed is seriously bad feng shui. You are charging the one place that is supposed to be for rest and intimacy with the static and complicated energy of extra bath towels, hoarded hotel shampoos, or old artwork. If you're not a great sleeper or are single and looking to partner up, check for clutter around your bed—your sex life depends on it! (Just kidding—kind of.)

- **Plastic dressers or drawers.** Anyone who has worked with us knows that we absolutely despise plastic dressers. These are the stepsiblings of under-the-bed bins but deserve to be discussed on their own. These microdressers are a good lightweight placeholder for the college student who moves dorms every few months but always has a tiny closet. But when adults own them, these bins often become a holding pen for junk that should be tossed. Clutter attracts more clutter. And these shoddily made bins, which easily come off kilter and are challenging to open and close, are essentially a clutter magnet. We'll say this: we've never come across a set of plastic drawers while working with a client and not donated or recycled at least 80 percent of the contents.

- **Specialized hangers and organization tools.** We're looking at you, shoe rack for twenty pairs of high heels no taller than three inches, jewelry case the size of a small dresser, and forty-loop scarf holder. All these things create singularly utilizable space that encourages us to have far more than we need or want. Think about it: if you have room for fifty pairs of earrings in your jewelry case and only have five pairs you love, wouldn't it feel a bit sad or weird to look at such an empty box? Wouldn't you want to go out and buy something to make the box look more full and beautiful? Instead, choose just what you love and then find the proper (smaller) storage afterward.

- **Super high shelves.** Cary's favorite thing about Kyle (besides her impeccable style and side-splitting jokes) is that she introduced Cary to her philosophy on tall storage: "If you can't easily reach it, it should be empty or used for deep storage or for decoration." If you can't reach it, what if you pretended it didn't exist?

- **Storage units.** We will venture to say, if you don't use it often enough to keep it in your primary residence, you don't need it. Most people rarely access their storage units, keeping in them the things they've saved "just in case"—items people often end up repurchasing if they are actually needed. Consider what life might be like without the things in storage—specialty items or things you use only once a year, items from past generations that no one uses. Ask yourself whether you would even notice if these items all went missing. Are you holding on to extra flatware for some unforeseeable future when you might need a dining table that seats twelve? Consider the costs, financial and otherwise, of holding all these items in a temperature-controlled, padlocked purgatory. The biggest difference you would notice if you removed storage units from your life would be more money in the bank and greater peace of mind.

NEW MINIMALISM
DESIGN PRINCIPLES

You can look forward to even more design advice in Chapter 7, where we will describe our twelve design principles. Honed over years of practice, these truths create an orderly yet inspired home. But sit tight for now, because you still need to take action on the actual decluttering process to make space for those design decisions.

PART II:

The Practice

It is so important to seed our
environments with things that speak
to us and support us in all we are
capable of being. —*Xorin Balbes*

CHAPTER 5

The Process

In the very act of exploring this topic of "too much," we have much to be grateful for. For not only are our basic needs being met, but we have an *overabundance* of items—so much so that we need to release some of them. While this feeling of clutter is overwhelming, the circumstance that got us here—abundance— is something to be truly thankful for. Oftentimes we see guilt associated with having too much, or feelings of shame or waste- fulness at having purchased something and now being faced with donating that very same item. Whatever the reason, we request that you remove all guilt associated with the act of declutter- ing and shift your focus to the *solution*. We want you to under- stand the problem and then take action. Forgive yourself of your past purchasing mistakes. What is important is to observe and *learn* from the behaviors that don't serve you and consequently change those behaviors for the better.

The key to making the decluttering process feel easy and light is to exercise gratitude. We focus on gratitude because it helps root us and makes us feel calm as we enter this process. It is an antidote to anxiety, fear, and shame. Guilt dwells in the past. Gratitude grounds you in the present.

DECLUTTERING BY CATEGORY

The category-by-category approach has been part of the New Minimalism process from our very humble beginning. As opposed to decluttering a specific area of your home, like your bedroom, you start with decluttering an entire category of your belongings, like your wardrobe. By gathering items within the same category from all areas of your home, you ensure that you fully understand the sheer volume of items you have in a particular category, and you don't have to backtrack to a category you thought was complete once you move into a new room.

For example, if you ignore the category-by-category approach and you begin with the clothes only in your bedroom, you will fail to account for the extra boots you have stored in the attic or the gardening clothes you keep in the garage. Then you may miss the opportunity to use the favorite college T-shirt you never wear to replace your falling-apart, ill-fitting gardening shirt.

With the category-by-category method, all items are accounted for and duplicates are revealed.

Additionally, the category-by-category approach allows you to have laser-like focus on a group of specific items in your home, helping you to stay on track and not become distracted by the multitude of categories that may exist within each room of your home.

Below are the categories that we have found in the typical American home and the order in which you should declutter them:

- Wardrobe and Accessories
- Kitchen and Entertaining
- Household Supplies and Toiletries
- Paperwork and Home Office
- Hobbies, Sports, and Toys
- Sentimental Items and Keepsakes
- Decor and Furniture

THERE IS NO "AWAY"

In 2006, Cary was living in Phnom Penh, the capital of Cambodia. In the bustling developing city, where survival far outweighs aesthetics, she drove by a huge open-air garbage dump every day. The trash was spilling into the surrounding streets, into the homes of villagers, into the mouths of livestock, and into the hands of local children, who used this garbage as their play toys. One morning, as she sat sidesaddle on the back of a beat-up moto-taxi and prepared to hold her breath as she passed the mountain of trash, it struck her. *There is no such thing as "away."*

What she meant was that in the United States we use this euphemism for what we do with garbage: we throw it "away." What Cary realized so clearly at that moment was that there is no mythical place called "away." Instead, these things we used to own end up at the garbage dump, in our oceans, or in someone else's backyard. Meanwhile, in her sustainable-design classes, Kyle was learning the technical term for this—a *closed-loop system*.

And while the casualness with which perfectly good items are thrown away is astonishing, we have discovered another interesting phenomenon. For our clients here in eco-conscious Northern California, the desire to *not* be wasteful causes them to become overwhelmed by clutter. They hold on to things they neither love nor use because they cannot bear to send something of value into the landfill. We get it. Yet having something sit in a box in your garage isn't really honoring it either.

We have a solution: donate. Donate all usable goods to the places that need them most. Yes, it's an extra step, but it is so worth it. Donating changes the entire feeling of letting something go. It's a true service, an act of deep compassion toward your community. And perhaps most importantly, it is one of the best things that you can do for the environment. At the end of this book we will provide you with resources to make the donation process as easy as possible. All that matters for now is that you agree to try!

START WITH THE WARDROBE

When discussing a project with a client, we first ask about the biggest pain points, the parts of the home that are the most frustrating and cause the most stress. In response, a client will typically describe the *rooms* that are giving her trouble. It's our job to clarify which *categories* exist in the spaces, because it is the items in the room, not the room itself, that contribute to the chaos.

For example, a client might say, "I don't know—the master bedroom is driving me crazy." So we inquire further: What types of items are in that room? She then describes the clothing piled on the chair, the coffee mugs that always end up on the bedside table, and the toiletries on top of the dresser. So now we can visualize how several different categories have made their way into the master bedroom. We will begin our first session by decluttering the client's clothing. During the next session we will tackle the kitchen (and find proper systems for those mugs), and

the third session is devoted to toiletries and household supplies (finally creating space in the bathroom so that the dresser top remains clear).

All of this is to say that while you may feel overwhelmed by *everything* in your home, you have to start somewhere. While the entire master bedroom will not feel completely transformed after your first decluttering session, you will have solved your wardrobe problems, contributing to peacefulness and harmony every time you get dressed in the morning, go to sleep at night, do your laundry, and shop for clothes. That's a pretty big impact! You will eventually get to all the categories in your home. Just start, and know that the process takes time.

During a decluttering session we ask a lot of questions. We look at items through a variety of lenses to help our clients determine whether items are adding value to their lives (and should stay) or are no longer relevant or needed (and should be donated).

Some of these questions include:

- Is this a duplicate?
- If you needed it, could you use something else in its place?
- Would you buy it again if it cost twice as much?
- And the ever-popular (yet not always effective, for reasons we are about to explain) question: Do you love it?

Let's imagine we are helping a client declutter her handbags (feel free to replace "handbags" with whatever category is most relevant to you). After staging all the bags, we hold up the first one. Our client responds, "I love that bag. I use it all the time." OK, we put it in the "keep" pile. We hold up a second bag, and again the client says, "I love that bag. I use it all the time." OK, "keep" pile. Fast-forward to twelve handbags later, and our client has said the same thing for all twelve bags.

OK, wait a minute. Do you really love all twelve handbags? And use them all the time? First of all, it is physically impossible to use all twelve handbags all the time. So let's just remove this answer from the table.

Secondly, what about the true meaning of *love*? Merriam-Webster's Collegiate Dictionary defines the verb to love as "to hold dear." In this light, is it possible to truly love even one handbag? Like *actually* love it, in the way you love your grandmother? Or your kids? Or your dog or cat? Would you do anything for this handbag?

When you use a word like *love* to describe all your handbags, how is it possible to differentiate between them? What if it came down to having just two and only two? If your house were on fire and you could grab only two handbags on the way out, which ones would make the cut? (Never mind the fact that if your house were actually on fire, we're guessing you would ditch the handbags altogether and save the family photos!)

Japanese decluttering master Marie Kondo says that if an item "sparks joy," it has earned the right to stay in your life. And while that lens may work for some people, others first need to define what *joy* means for themselves. Doing so requires a grounded self-awareness that won't work for the people who claim to love everything they own.

So let's say you are decluttering on your own, and you find yourself thinking that you love all your items. What do you do then? At this point, you have to pivot and look at your things through a different lens. You have to be *even more discerning*. You start by slowing down, taking a deep breath, and stepping back. Reexamine your use of the word *love*. Give it back the power it was originally intended to have and be selective when using it in your day-to-day life.

Because here's the thing—even if you love something, you can still donate it! We know—it's shocking! It is possible to concurrently appreciate the beauty and craftsmanship of an item and let someone else own it. The act of cherishing an item and donating it are not mutually exclusive; in fact, those two acts, at their heart, are probably positively correlated.

Things are made to be used, and when they are not being used, you are not honoring their inherent usefulness, the time and energy it took to extract those resources, dye the fabric, produce the zippers, and assemble the materials. So if you truly love your twelfth-favorite handbag, you'll understand that you are not using it with the frequency it deserves, and you'll donate it so it becomes someone else's first favorite handbag.

HOW LONG WILL
THIS TAKE, ANYWAY?

A good rule of thumb is that each major category will take a full day to completely declutter. Of course, this varies depending on the size of your home, the quantity of items in each category, and the speed with which you make decisions. Note: the clearer your vision of the home and life you want to create for yourself, the faster you will be at sorting your things (which explains why the first half of this book is dedicated to this topic). For example, if you know that as a busy career person who works long hours and travels frequently you need a home that is a sanctuary and a place of respite, then anything in your home that does not contribute to a feeling of total relaxation and peace or is not a daily essential should obviously be donated!

What's important here is to keep up momentum and commit to completing the category once the sorting begins. The last thing we want is for you to empty out your entire closet or kitchen cabinets, get overwhelmed, and then quit halfway through. Know in advance that lulls in energy will happen. Instead of shoving piles of sweaters back into your closet willy-nilly, take fifteen to twenty minutes to go out for a walk, make a cup of coffee, watch cat videos, or do anything else that will reinvigorate you and help you achieve clarity.

HOW TO
PREPARE FOR A
DECLUTTERING
SESSION

- **Set a date.** Yes, you may have to declutter on a Saturday, and yes, a social event will likely surface to tempt you to do anything but declutter that day. Grandma needs help changing a light bulb? You're there! Resist the urge to convince yourself that it would be better to declutter "next weekend," which will turn into "later," which will turn into never. Pick a date and stick to it.
- **Have an assistant.** Enlist the help of a friend, a family member, or anyone whose opinion you value and who is committed to assisting you from start to finish. Having a second pair of hands will make the process so much faster. Plus, having someone

else present will keep you from entering the black hole of nostalgia and memories that emerges when you sort your things. How will you trick someone into helping you in this way? Make it more appealing by providing lunch and snacks. Or pay them cold, hard cash (hey, time is money). Or find a friend who wants to declutter his or her own life, and take turns assisting each other. Whatever you do, make sure you have someone to help, because an assistant holds you accountable and is imperative for a successful day.

- **Have cleaning products on hand.** Grab a broom, a dustpan, rags, and our all-purpose cleaning solution (see page 113). Even the most pristine homes have secret dust bunny colonies.

- **Have lunch already prepared.** Whether you grab lunch from a nearby café or have leftovers ready to heat up, having a lunch plan in place will be important when your brain is tired from so much decision making.

- **Make sure all laundry is complete and dishes are clean.** The point of all of this is to make space for the most-used items in your home, and those items are probably the ones that you've recently worn or used to cook last night's dinner. This is an imperative first step we recommend completing the day before your session.

- **Gather all those shopping bags and old boxes that you keep saving for a rainy day.** These bags are perfect for gathering your donations. For the kitchen session, you will likely need cardboard boxes and newspaper for the fragile items.

- **Plan your donation strategy.** If you don't already have go-to organizations where you like to donate, take a minute to check out the Resources section at the end of the book and research a few places in your area. If you don't have a plan for donations, it's easy to lose momentum at the end of a long day and let the bags languish in your home or car.

TAKE ACTION: If you don't have a stash of bags on hand (which would make you perhaps the first person ever), we have a special New Minimalism secret: go to your local hardware store and pick up a pack of lawn-trimming bags. These extra-large brown paper bags are typically used for yard waste. They are huge, earth friendly, and extremely efficient, especially for clothes, bedding, towels, or any other soft goods. Please avoid at all costs buying plastic garbage bags for your decluttering tasks! These bags end up straight in the landfill after briefly shuttling your items from the car to the donation center.

HURRAY, IT'S DECLUTTERING DAY!

We recommend starting first thing in the morning, right after a hearty breakfast and a little caffeine. Don't neglect the setting: turn on the lights, open the blinds, crack the windows to circulate fresh air, perhaps turn on some background music. And drink water! A couple of hours into sorting, these little tips will massively help your productivity and focus. Use your assistant to keep things organized as you rapidly sort your belongings. And remember, take a lunch break when you need it. Note: you are ready for lunch if/when your stomach growls audibly and/or you lose track of your thoughts midsentence.

Staging

The importance of staging cannot be stressed enough. By removing items from the context of where they have been living in your home, it is easier to view them with an objective eye. Here are our staging recommendations:

- **Designate a staging area.** In a room near the items to be sorted, clear all the surfaces, push the furniture aside, and create a clearing to stage your items (e.g., a dining table works great for staging kitchen items). You will use this space for the sorting process.

OATH OF A GOOD ASSISTANT

I am here to support and help my friend.

I am the muscle; I will keep piles organized and tidy as the decision making rapidly progresses.

I will give my unbiased opinion but only when solicited.

I will use a timer and set sorting goals so that we stay on track.

- **Gather all the items in the category from every part of your home.** For your wardrobe, for example, empty your closet entirely, remove all items from the dresser, the hall closet, under the bed, the basement, et cetera. Bring all clothing to the staging area.
- **In the staging area, place like items with like items.** You are not deciding what stays and what will be donated just yet. You are solely grouping all your sweaters together, placing all your shoes in one corner, stacking all your T-shirts into one pile.
- **Pause and take it all in.** Once all items are in the staging area, take a step back and look at everything. Did you realize that you had six pairs of nearly identical black boots or forty concert T-shirts? This is your reality check.
- **Clean.** Return to the now-empty spaces in your home and give them a thorough sweep. Wipe them down using a rag and our all-purpose cleaning solution (see page 113). Use our wood polish (see page 115) to give your wooden pieces the love and respect they deserve.
- **Strategize.** With everything now removed from the space, try viewing it with fresh eyes. Use this time to consider your overall organization strategy. Can you decrease your wardrobe so that it takes up only half of the closet? Can you commit to keeping the floor space under your bed clear? What if you display your jewelry inside your closet rather than keep it in a tangled mess on top of your dresser?
- **Set a goal for yourself.** As you appreciate the beauty of your now-empty space, consider what percentage of items needs

to be donated so that the room can breathe again. 30 percent? 40 percent? 75 percent? Give yourself a benchmark to keep yourself on track during the sorting process.

- **Go back to the pile of items to be decluttered and select your favorites.** From all the items laid out before you, cherry-pick your five favorite pieces and place them on display (maybe you can hang them from a door or set them on a side table). These items epitomize your aesthetic or personal style and will subsequently act as your guiding light.
- **Designate your sorting piles.** Write the following categories on sticky notes or directly on the bags you will use to sort your belongings:
  - Keep
  - Donate
  - Maybe—this includes clothing items to be tried on. Refrain from pausing the process every time you need to try something on. Save this for the end.
  - Recycle
  - Trash
  - To-do. This includes all the items that:
    1 belong to someone else and need to be returned,
    2 need repair or special cleaning,
    3 need to be returned to a store, or
    4 you want to sell at a consignment shop.

Sorting

This is where all the decision making comes in. Start with an area that holds less emotional attachment for you. For example, if you feel super attached to all your shoes, start with your jackets. You want to begin with an area where you can swiftly make progress.

For clarity on the life you are creating for yourself, go back and read your top values from the journaling exercise about finding your "why" (see page 29). The clearer you are on the life you want, the more decisive you will be when sorting your possessions.

It sounds silly, but keeping the bags near you as you sort makes a big difference in time. You don't want to walk halfway across the room every time you need to put an item in the donation pile. Follow the steps below to sort your items with assembly-line efficiency:

- **First, look at the five favorite items you've set aside.** Remember to use these items to guide your decisions. Everything you keep should be able to hold its own next to these items.
- **Pick up each individual object, one at a time.** (Yes, every single item.)
- **As you hold each item, tap into your gut reactions, your first impulse.** Notice what excites you. On the other hand, notice if you repeatedly validate *why* something should stay.

- **Place item in the appropriate pile.**
- **If you're unsure how to decide on a certain item, ask yourself the following questions:** Does this item make me feel like a goddess, a warrior, the most brilliant person in the room, or the best version of myself? Would I seek out a special repair person to fix this item should something happen to it?
- **Listen to your assistant!** It can be challenging to maintain objectivity when considering certain belongings that have seen you through the trials and tribulations of life. Use the perspective of your assistant. For example, when your assistant tells you that your grandfather's dusty golf hat has seen better days or your third pair of summer sandals seems a little excessive, donate these items. Your assistant is there to help.
- **Keep a list of "holes."** A decluttered lifestyle requires workhorse, go-to items that are well made and can function across various scenarios. With this in mind, it is possible that during the process you will discover that a certain key piece is missing. For example, you love wearing jeans, but you have twelve pairs of jeans that all fail in a certain way: too wide in the waist, too worn in the knees, unflattering color. Donate these garments and write "badass jeans" on your list. You're more likely to actually replace the item if you remove the failing pieces from the premises. At the end of the day, you'll have a short list of items on which to focus your attention and resources. Armed with this list, you will be less likely to make impulsive, less-than-perfect purchases when shopping.
- **As you make decisions on large sections of the category, start to put things back where they belong.** This will be a trial-and-error part of the day. Finished sorting shirts? Place your "keep" shirts in the space where you think they will work best. As you continue to work through more items, you may find that your shirts would actually work best somewhere else. Play around with the arrangement. You can look forward to specific design tips in Chapter 7.

TAKE ACTION: When in doubt during the decision-making process, reference your favorite items to assess whether the item in question aligns with them. This step allows you to focus on the items that best serve you in your present day, making it easier to release old items related to outdated ideas about yourself. Remember the wise words of stylist Stacy London: "Dress for yourself and what suits your lifestyle, and you will always look good."

OK, you finished the major round of sorting! Three or four hours may have passed, and you are doing great! What's next? Addressing the "maybe" pile.

The truth about the maybe pile is that if an item made its way there to begin with, it's safe to say you can donate it. It's just like the awkward stage in a relationship before breaking up; you care for that T-shirt, you've had fun times together, but the color is a little off and the fit is a little too . . . something. You know something isn't quite right. Dragging it out only makes the inevitable harder. Donate!

TAKE ACTION: Keep a discerning eye on the "to-do" pile as the day progresses. Make sure it doesn't become so gargantuan that it will likely never be completed. Here's a helpful trick when evaluating the to-do pile: How many hours will it take to complete all these tasks, including travel to and from each location and time spent there? If you were to give yourself an hourly rate, would it be worth your time to complete these tasks? If the tasks amount to four hours of effort on your part, is it worth your hourly rate times four to complete? Food for thought.

WRAP IT UP

Build at least one hour into the end of the day to wrap up all loose ends. At this time you will undoubtedly be tempted to kick off your shoes, grab a mug of tea (or something stronger), and relax on the couch, but finishing your session with your home clear of items to be dealt with is worth the effort. Complete the following steps to wrap up your day:

- **Examine your to-do pile.** Does it feel exciting or daunting? Be assertive and discerning, because it's entirely counterproductive for you to be left with hours of projects to deal with at the end of the day! Use your newfound ruthlessness to donate the items that you are wavering over.
- **Return the borrowed items to their original owners.** When considering the borrowed items in your to-do pile, ask yourself whether the owner has been requesting the item back. Who knows, maybe the owner would rather you donate it with the rest of your haul. It doesn't hurt to call and ask.
- **Bring your donation pile to your local donation center.** If you don't already have a go-to donation locale, check the Resources section at the end of the book for tips.
- **Schedule a time in your calendar for any remaining tasks.** Really! Take out your calendar, sit down, and find a day to complete these tasks.

- **Kick back and unwind.** We recommend commemorating a job well done by savoring a quiet, easy evening, whether that means taking a shower, going out for a casual dinner, or cuddling up with a cup of tea or a glass of wine. Treat yourself!

What if you've decluttered and your items still don't fit well within the space? Now is the time to be honest with yourself. Either you have the world's smallest space—so small even Harry Potter would feel sorry for you—and you need to obtain additional storage, or your purge is not yet complete. For most people, the latter situation is the case.

"Wait, but look at how much I've gotten rid of!" you might say. Yes, this is wonderful, but try not to focus on how much is leaving. What's important is what is *staying* and whether it will work in your space *today*. Don't feel sad or embarrassed—you showed up and did great work. Sometimes you simply need time to go through this process in phases. Schedule a check-in date in three months to reassess this category. By that time you will be well acquainted with the first step in living more simply, and your priorities will become even clearer. There are sure to be items you have found during that three-month period that you don't need and now are easy to donate!

CHAPTER 6

Category by Category

A note on archetypes: You'll see symbols representing the four archetypes next to the decluttering categories listed in this chapter. These symbols are meant to call attention to the archetypes that notoriously have trouble with particular categories. This is a call to be extra mindful and compassionate with yourself through a specific category of decluttering if the symbol representing your archetype appears next to it. It is also a call to review the tips we've provided for you in Chapter 3 and keep them close at hand.

WARDROBE + ACCESSORIES

Most-Affected Archetypes: Connected, Frugal, Practical

Diana had an entire walk-in closet (and half of another closet) filled with all kinds of clothing: an unending collection of jeans, collared work shirts, beachwear, flowing dresses, and shorts. Diana said that she dreaded each morning before work, when she would look into her packed closets, feel totally overwhelmed, and then just panic and grab the same black sweater and skirt she wore all the time. Even when she had time to get dressed before parties or nights out, she struggled with creating outfits, not remembering how the rarely worn clothes fit, what they matched with, how she felt wearing them. These closets were packed with items she wasn't sure about—clothes that were old and outdated for her body and her current personal style.

Here is the place where we can't help but expound one of our favorite philosophies: the myth of choice. Somewhere in our cultural evolution toward a consumer-heavy lifestyle, some great advertising goddess came up with the brilliant idea that more is better. This idea has become so ingrained in our American ethos that we believe having more options liberates us and allows us to be our most fulfilled and most creative selves. Even that language—liberty and creativity—is at the very core of what we've always held to be the cornerstone of enlightened civilization.

Yet it has been proven that having more choices does the exact opposite of giving us freedom. It leads us to feel overwhelmed, unsatisfied, and confused. Think of an artist given a warehouse full of every medium and supply she could ever want. Ask her to make something beautiful, and she'll be totally paralyzed. But then think of an artist handed a single piece of paper, her favorite fine-point marker, a roll of tape, and a pair of scissors. If you give her the same assignment, her creativity will be tested, challenged, and explored within the confines of these supplies.

So when we asked Diana to pull out the five items she loved the most and felt like her best self in, we were surprised to see a huge smile on her face as she jumped up and grabbed a couple of conservatively cut, immaculately fitting sheath dresses. With no hesitation, she told us how these dresses made her feel: instantly pulled together and sexy without feeling overly revealed. This combination made her feel confident and powerful, which were great attributes for her professional life. She wore these dresses to work and to industry events, and then with a quick change of shoes and the addition of lipstick, they turned into her favorite date-night clothes.

As we continued sorting Diana's clothing items one at a time, we ended up with a "keep" pile of about twelve sheath dresses, three pairs of go-to jeans, ten luxurious sweaters of various weights, and a drawer's worth of yoga clothing. If a total stranger were to see that "keep" pile, every item would make sense. And if you knew Diana (as we came to) you would note that each garment was quintessentially her: elegant cuts, quality fabrics, classic styles.

The beauty of having such a clear sense of style and an awareness of which clothes made her feel the best was that it was equally clear which items should be donated. Each and every one of the garments she donated was, in one way or another, not her. By the end of the session, we had bagged over 70 percent of her former wardrobe to be donated to Dress for Success and Goodwill, thereby creating space to welcome her husband's wardrobe back into the master closet.

Diana estimated that even with all these items leaving, it would hardly change what she wore on a daily basis. The biggest impact would be that now, when she got dressed every morning, it would be effortless and joyful. She could look into her closet—which now had the appearance of a high-end boutique—and feel grateful for all her garments, which were draped carefully from matching hangers. For Diana, it was never a matter of having more but of removing the noise so that she could pay attention to the items that made her feel like her best, most honest, and most fulfilled self.

DECLUTTERING YOUR WARDROBE

We begin the decluttering process with clothing for reasons both logical and philosophical. Logically, we begin with the wardrobe because letting go of clothing will open up valuable space in the core of your home, revealing storage you didn't know that you had, thus informing where other categories can possibly live. For example, in decluttering your wardrobe first, you may find that you have room to store your camping gear in the hall closet, whereas before the hall closet was stuffed with unused jackets, and your beloved camping gear was relegated to an off-site storage unit. Or because you no longer need a shoe rack, you now have room to store your travel bag in your primary closet, making packing for a weekend getaway a breeze.

Philosophically, we begin with the wardrobe because it's a personal category—meaning we don't yet need to account for

BEFORE

AFTER

the opinions of others who may share your space. Clothing is also the foundation of your relationship to the material world. It is your second skin, it protects you from the elements, and it keeps you safe and warm. And if you are able to declutter, clarify, and simplify the items you use to protect and express yourself every day, you will strengthen your decluttering "muscle" at its core, and decluttering will become easier and easier as you progress into other areas of your home.

For your first foray into decluttering, keep the following tips in mind:

1 With your wardrobe, perhaps more than any other category, it's worth taking the time to curate your five favorite items.

2 Determine what it is about your favorites that you love so much. The cut? The fabric? The fact that you could practice yoga, go to a last-minute meeting, or go from work to a night out in them? Take note of how you feel in your favorite clothes. Let that be your standard for all other items.

3 You can get away with owning far less clothing than you do now. You don't have to turn into a person who lives out of a backpack and has just two T-shirts, but consider that you could be well and variably dressed with just ten items in your closet at any moment.

4 Before you dig into your maybe pile at the end of your sorting, take a look at the abundance and perfection of your "keep" pile. If the maybe pile is so large that it feels overwhelming to try it all on, do yourself a favor and pull only the very best to try on and donate the rest.

5 Don't go overboard with your to-dos. Do you really want to tailor an entire old wardrobe to suit your new body after you have a baby or attend boot camp? Or would purchasing a couple of quality items that fit you now make you feel even better?

KITCHEN + ENTERTAINING

Most-Affected Archetypes: Practical, Energetic

After you finish decluttering your wardrobe, your next decluttering day will be devoted to the kitchen. The kitchen is a particularly sacred place to us. As Krista Tippett says, "The family dinner embodies memory in communal time." This means that the experience of sitting down and spending time nourishing our bodies and relishing eating together is key to twenty-first-century American life but is also a deeper, primal yearning we've always had.

The abundance of goods following World War II gave rise to the newly minted virtue of *convenience*. The invention of the dishwasher meant that cleaning up after a meal required only the pressing of a few buttons, rather than being a vigorous chore. The benefits of this convenience, as well as those of the washing machine, the vacuum, and the microwave, were obvious in the rise of quality of life for women who'd previously been relegated to the never-ending physical chores of running the home. The downside of this progress was a speeding up of the pace of life and a disconnection from our physical world and each other.

The negative side effects of this speeding up were perhaps most pronounced in our food, which was now readily available in microwavable trays and easy-to-store aluminum cans. This convenience caused us to become detached from our bodily wisdom of what we so deeply desire: nourishment. As Krista Tippett so eloquently states in her book *Becoming Wise*, "As the era of careless food comes to a reckoning, we're relearning the astonishingly elemental delight in growing what we eat and preparing it as though it matters." The choices we make in the kitchen, just like the choices we make about our wardrobes, echo through our day and our communities.

We think often of our clients Taya and James when we think about nourishment and the kitchen. They were college sweethearts who had delighted in entertaining and hosting large dinner parties throughout their twenties. Taya was a talented and joyful cook, mastering complicated techniques and expanding

her range of international flavor profiles. And then life evolved into a family of four and two exciting, challenging careers for Taya and James.

Feeding two enthusiastic and rambunctious young girls after a full day of work began to feel like a draining chore to Taya. She struggled to create enough prep space on her counters, which were full of drying sippy cups, papers from school, and James's multitude of coffee-related apparatuses. Taya was deeply frustrated by the state of her kitchen, but upon digging deeper, we learned that what she was most upset by was the fact that meals were a throwaway part of her day, rather than the anchoring, pleasurable experience of the past. She had rationalized that it was impossible to spend two hours cooking when her girls had to be in bed just ninety minutes after she got home from work. So Taya, defeated, had given up on the idea of a family meal and instead opted for premade and frozen meals in plastic containers, cooked in the microwave.

During our kitchen session, Taya donated everything that was not a workhorse or a staple in her life. This created space on her counters so that they were ready at any moment for food preparation. As a result, her family's meals became more elemental yet somehow even more delicious. Olive oil, salt, and pepper became her standbys. Roasted vegetables and simply prepared meats became interesting with the variation in the seasons. With this simpler but more satisfying form of cooking, James and the girls were excited to help with meal preparation. The ritual of cooking, eating, and cleaning up after a family meal became the cornerstone of their evenings together. It promoted bodily well-being but also emotional health—connecting to one another and to their food.

TAKE ACTION: Bring your own jar (BYOJ). In cultivating this habit, you'll essentially never leave home without some kind of container. Kyle and Cary both alternate between simply using our water bottles (which we always have on us) or a mason jar. This jar serves as a personal, always-available reusable receptacle for any food or drink item you may purchase when out and about.

So far, we've used our jars for smoothies, acai bowls, coffee (like Philz Mint Mojito), tea, water, avocados, oatmeal, salad bar items, and freshly foraged berries, just to name a few. Keep the following tips in mind:

It's unimportant exactly what brand or style you use—to each his own. What does matter is that the jar is durable (it will be bouncing around in your backpack, bag, or bike pannier, after all) and that it has a lid that seals tightly (Cary's only purse still smells like cardamom on warm days from a slightly leaky jar of chai latte).

New habits undoubtedly require a little effort to establish. But the beauty of habits is their effortlessness—eventually they'll stop being work and start being second nature.

It takes a little bit of moxie to offer up your jar at restaurants, coffee shops, or grocery stores. Do it anyway. Avoiding the constant stream of disposables is better for the earth, and glass or aluminum containers are more pleasant to eat and drink out of and far easier to travel with than paper or plastic containers.

Each time you use a jar in public, you strengthen ecological awareness in your community. When you BYOJ, you not only ensure that far fewer products end up in our landfills (or recycling or compost facilities, which still require resources to run), but you also set a subtle example for your fellow consumers. You are one more person moving the needle, ever so slightly, toward environmental compassion and responsibility. And that small act means a lot.

DECLUTTERING YOUR KITCHEN

When you declutter your kitchen, look to see where there are some missed opportunities for fully utilizing the existing storage. Before you remove all the dishes from the cabinets, open all the doors and examine the space. Look at the positive and negative space. Positive space is where all things made of matter (for example, dishes) currently reside. Negative space is all the air in between. Do you have gaping holes of air in certain areas? Do your mugs have enough space above them that you could fit three more rows? If your shelves are adjustable, lucky you! You can customize the shelving to your specific needs. Make a mental note of where you have unused space and proceed with decluttering your kitchen.

We always estimate that a kitchen will take a full day to complete. Between the pantry (yes, it's time to finally get rid of those expired soups and spices), your daily and formal dishes, all your cookware, glasses, barware, utensils, and kitchen tools—well, it's a project. The good news? A single day of effort in your kitchen will not only make every single meal you cook from now on easier, it will also make you a better host and make the time you spend in your kitchen so much more pleasurable. So yeah, it's worth it!

The key to decluttering your kitchen is to prioritize the daily over the occasional. For 80 to 90 percent of your meals, you are likely using the same 10 to 20 percent of your cooking tools, pans, and dishes. If you give those essential tools plenty of space, meal prep and cooking will only be as difficult as your recipe, not as hard as finding all the tools you need!

Does your kitchen table fit only eight people? Keep eight plates and eight cups. Are you more of a beer or water drinker? Let go of that set of margarita glasses that hogs an entire shelf.

Other excellent objects to donate: anything that is bulky, overly specialized, or could easily (if not perfectly) be substituted with something else. For example, if you tend to cook stir-fry once a month or so, does giving your wok a full shelf to itself make sense? Could you make do with your large frying pan? Do you make enough heated sandwiches for a large countertop panini maker to be necessary? Or could that same frying pan work? If you're not much of a baker, could you get away with a simple whisk to handle your baking needs rather than a large stand mixer? The key here is to keep your countertops clear and to give plenty of physical and visual space to the objects you use every day. This will make your everyday life in your kitchen easier, cooking more appealing, and eating more pleasurable.

OUTSOURCING IN YOUR OWN COMMUNITY

There is great beauty in not having to do it all—particularly when you can support the talented chefs located right in your community instead. Rather than owning all the perfect, highly specific accoutrements to make a fancy Thai dinner, why not patronize the family-owned restaurant located in town? Rather than storing all the ingredients to bake a complicated French pastry, why not leave it to the experts and pick up a dessert from your local bakery? In doing so, you save time and release the need to have a million specialty ingredients and tools, plus you support local businesses. Win-win.

TAKE ACTION: After you are finished decluttering all your kitchen-related wares, put the items back according to priority of use. Is your daily coffee ritual more important than accessing your collection of tea boxes? What rule says that coffee and tea need to live together? Place the mugs and coffee accessories on a shelf where they are easily accessible, perhaps sacrificing the ease with which you can reach the tea boxes and the ceremonial matcha tea set. By putting items back according to priority, you'll make sure that your most utilized items are also your most accessible.

Continue to add the items back into the cabinets and drawers according to priority, adjusting your shelves as you go, building from the bottom up. Lower each shelf to decrease the amount of negative space above each row of dishes. If you can't adjust your shelves or it doesn't make sense to, employ a simple shelf divider to decrease the amount of open space. Maybe that shelf divider that you intended to use in the laundry room but never did could be used in the kitchen instead? If you don't come across a shelf divider by the end of the decluttering process, add it to your list of things to purchase.

HOUSEHOLD SUPPLIES + TOILETRIES

Most-Affected Archetypes:
Frugal, Practical

The first time we opened the cabinets under the sink in Sofia's large kitchen, we were shocked. Like so many of our clients, she was a successful working professional. She had a lovely, updated kitchen with an abundance of built-in storage, great natural light, and gorgeous finishes. Yet her space had become dysfunctional and hard to maintain because it was overflowing with stuff. Under the sink there were piles of highly specific cleaning products assigned to all areas of her home (granite countertops or wooden countertops, appliances, sinks, toilet bowls, mirrors and windows, linens, et cetera). As you would expect, it was nearly impossible to find the stainless steel appliance wipes among the hoards of cleaning supplies, so inevitably Sofia went out and bought duplicates.

This habit of overbuying was not limited to the cleaning products. She also had drawers upon drawers of personal hygiene, beauty, and grooming products. From the five different types of shampoo and conditioner in her shower to the bins of hair sprays, brushes, and tools, Sofia had a seemingly infinite number of possible hair routines. As for makeup products, Beyoncé's backup dancers probably had less.

We've discussed how having too many choices is a detriment to happiness and contentment, but the state of Sofia's home further highlighted two frightening trends in our culture today. The first is the meteoric rise of hyperspecialized products. The abundance of products on the market leads people to believe they need a litany of items to keep even a simple studio apartment clean or to solve all their beauty, skin, hair, and nail woes. Not only is this expensive and crazy making when you clean your home or get ready in the morning, but it also supports the idea that you need to test several products before finding your perfect match. This is what Sofia was suffering from. When we asked Sofia whether she could get rid of the half-used shampoo bottles, she went into detail about her systematic shampoo-rotating schedule. OK, our mission was clear. It was our job to show Sofia that approaching life in this way was a huge time suck and energy drain. Exactly how much time do you want to devote to keeping track of which shampoo brand has what effect on your hair? And given that she employed this strategy with her shampoo, you can imagine what her skin-care routine was like.

It appeared that Sofia was using this testing idea as an excuse to keep a lot of things, and a way to fill her days and make her feel as though she was being productive and busy, even down to the tiniest details of her daily routine. We introduced Sofia to the idea that she could still test shampoos if she bought one at a time. This requires making a decision about what type you will try and either using up the whole bottle or, if you are not satisfied with the results, moving on to the next type. Dumping a half bottle of shampoo down the drain is indeed wasteful. And to that point, we urged Sofia to use an entire bottle before moving on to the next. But in her particular case, the first step toward a simpler self-care routine was removing the excess choices of half-used products that had accumulated over time. And in service of a simple beauty and home-cleaning routine, that might be where you should start, too.

Another trend we have encountered in the category of household supplies and toiletries is a fixation on "cleanliness." You know, John Wesley said, "Cleanliness is indeed next to godliness" in 1778, before indoor plumbing was common, sewage-treatment systems had been implemented, or much-needed vaccines for contagious diseases had been developed. We've taken the idea of being squeaky clean a bit too far, as if it equates to being proper and good. As though unless your grout is sparkling white, it is not clean. Did you know that your originally white grout can have a slight yellowish tinge and still be "clean"? Stained and clean are two separate properties that *can* coexist.

Fake fragrances, harsh cleansers, and chemical dyes are often wrongly associated with the idea of "clean." When in reality they all combine to create a medley of health-harming toxins that we

then subject ourselves to on a daily basis. A clean home should smell fresh and natural like the outdoors, or like nothing at all.

We've been misled to believe that a clean home requires the sanitation of an operating room. Yet scientists are continuing to find that hypercleanliness is not healthy for us (it's bad for our immune systems and can make us more susceptible to allergies). We won't get into the details of decoding the ingredients list of your beauty and cleaning products. Rather than worry about which chemicals are bad for you, what if you simply try to eliminate most of them in the first place? There are very few things that white vinegar, baking soda, or lemon juice can't fix (and what we find astonishing is that these basic cleaning products are nowhere to be found in the cleaning aisle of the grocery store!).

What's more, the not-so-subtle message behind advertising that every part of your body needs a different soap, that your hair requires a half dozen solutions, and that your face needs twenty products to be presentable is that we are flawed, ugly, not good enough. That we must constantly wage battle against the never-ending slide toward dirtiness and aging. This, my friends, is total bullshit. This message disconnects us from the actual core of what it is to be human. To be fully human is inherently to be messy. In missing out on those chances to show up as your completely human and vulnerable self, you miss out on the chance to experience the deep connections, growth, creativity, and fullness that are our birthrights. To be clear, we're not suggesting that people stop washing and cleaning up entirely, letting grime and grease build up everywhere—gross. Our main point is that by maintaining a basic standard of cleanliness and adhering to a minimal beauty routine will make your life more simple and stress free, and you don't need to feel bad about yourself in the process.

Through our work, Sofia learned that the best home-cleaning routine is low maintenance. She was able to get rid of her collection of specialty cleaning products and settle on using a basic eco-friendly all-purpose cleaner. She came to understand that her exhaustive list of beauty product choices was sucking up her valuable time and was able to settle on selecting one type of shampoo. She was already health conscious and environmentally concerned; she wanted to honor the planet and her body by using fewer toxins—she just needed a little push in the right direction.

TAKE ACTION: Before decluttering your toiletries and household supplies, do some quick research to see whether a local church, homeless shelter, or women's shelter has use for your unopened items. Women's shelters are often in need of toiletries.

DECLUTTERING YOUR HOUSEHOLD SUPPLIES + TOILETRIES

Just as with any category, we begin by removing all items from where they're currently stored in the home. We recommend starting with household-cleaning products and then moving on to toiletries in a separate round. When deciding which cleaning products to keep, default to removing nearly everything you've been using, except for the following:

- White vinegar
- Baking soda
- Castile soap
- Essential oils (lemon and lavender are good places to start)
- Lemon juice
- Jojoba oil (for wood polish)

Yes, that's it! You can clean your whole house with this list. So what do you do with all your cleaning products that aren't on this list? You might think you should give them to other people to use. But then you are just exposing other people to the same toxins that you are trying to avoid. We hate to advocate against reuse, but the best action in this case is to safely dispose of the products and then start fresh with the list above. Cleaning products that are water soluble are safe to dilute with water and pour down the drain (use rubber gloves to protect your hands, wear glasses to protect your eyes, and avoid directly inhaling fumes). For products like furniture polish and oven cleaner, you'll need to research safe disposal practices. Your local waste-management company—you know, the people who pick up your trash—usually has customer service representatives who are quite knowledgeable and helpful on the subject. And finally, please stop buying those scented trash bags! Covering the scent of trash with a different scent of fake flowers and potpourri is fooling no one (despite what the commercials say) but might be what is giving you a headache.

Now, on to sorting toiletries and beauty products. Remove all your skin-care, makeup, first-aid, and travel-sized products from all their hiding places around the home, including your bathroom, suitcases, guest bathrooms, and so on. If you don't have a large counter in the bathroom to stage the items, use a folding table or your kitchen table (cover it with newspapers first). Pro tip: use a large bin to efficiently shuttle everything to your staging table. Place every item on this surface, lining up like items with like items.

Evaluate all the items in front of you. How many are duplicates? How many items are super specialized or require a detailed application process? How many are half-full and have been for a while? Get rid of them! By the end of this process, all that ought to remain are the basic toiletries you use each and every day. One shampoo and one conditioner, one face wash, one body soap, one lotion. If you wear makeup, test out a basic daily makeup routine—something like mascara, lip balm, and a bit of blush (Cary's daily routine), or eyebrow pencil and tinted moisturizer (Kyle's). Much like simplifying your wardrobe, simplifying your bath and beauty regimens guarantees another easy, effortless portion of your day. Farmers' markets are great sources for locally made soaps and natural beauty products.

After you decide which items you're ready to part with, first see what you can donate (see Take Action on page 110). As for the opened items that you decide you don't need, rinse these water-soluble products down the drain and recycle the bottles (to save water, fill the sink with warm water, let the bottles soak with their tops off to loosen their contents, then rinse out each bottle). If it's painful to see your dollars go down the drain, take that as a lesson and use it to make better purchasing decisions moving forward.

When out in the world, avoid freebies and handouts at all costs. You don't have to accept a freebie just because someone offers one to you. Thanks but no thanks!

RECIPE: ALL-PURPOSE CLEANING SOLUTION

Surprise! You don't need a separate cleaner for every surface in your home. Our all-purpose cleaning solution can be used all over the house, for everything from floors to windows to countertops. And fear not, the vinegar smell goes away once the solution dries. This works way better than any glass cleaner you will find in the store—no streaks. Plus, no harsh scents or scary chemicals!

INGREDIENTS

1 cup water
1 cup white vinegar
Juice of 1 small lemon
2 to 3 drops of essential oil
(omit the oil if you are using
to clean glass)

DIRECTIONS

• Use an empty spray bottle to combine the water and the vinegar.
• Add the lemon juice.
• Add a few drops of your favorite essential oil—tea tree, lavender, and peppermint all work great.

RECIPE: SIMPLE AND SAFE MIRACLE SCRUB

There is great peace of mind that comes from taking a shower and knowing that there are no toxic chemicals rising up in the steam all around you.

INGREDIENTS

2 tablespoons nontoxic
dish soap
½ cup baking soda
1 to 2 tablespoons water

DIRECTIONS

• In a small, shallow container (food-storage containers work great), combine the dish soap and the baking soda.
• Slowly add the water to create a paste.
• Scrub soap scum away! This is great for scrubbing toilets, too.
• Rinse with warm water.

RECIPE: HOMEMADE WOOD POLISH

Use this simple polish as an alternative to aerosol spray cans and petroleum-based products. (We found this recipe at www .care2.com/greenliving/alternative-furniture-polish.html.)

INGREDIENTS

10 drops lemon essential oil

2 tablespoons lemon juice

2 to 5 drops jojoba oil
(this oil won't go rancid in
warm conditions)

DIRECTIONS

• In a small glass container, mix all ingredients.

• Dip a soft cotton rag into the mixture and use it to wipe down wood furniture. Be sparing in your application.

MORE CLEANING TIPS

To replace the need for paper towels, keep an abundance of cotton rags on hand. Don't be afraid to use them liberally while cleaning. Kyle ends up using four to five medium-sized rags when cleaning her small bathroom.

Microfiber cloths are great for dusting.

For a little sanity when it comes time to do laundry, we recommend keeping a separate laundry bin for all household linens, like sheets, bath towels, kitchen towels, and cleaning rags.

If you have cleaning professionals clean your home and are wondering what to do since they use their own products, the solution is still to create your own natural cleaning products and then instruct your cleaning professionals to use them. You will be doing their health a favor, as well!

PAPERWORK + HOME OFFICE

Most-Affected Archetypes: Practical, Frugal, Energetic

Decluttering your home office and paperwork can be a challenging task mainly because it is such a dense area of the home. Each piece of paper, while deceptively small in size, relates to a larger task—for example, the credit card you've been meaning to cancel, the bill that needs to be paid, the note that needs responding to, the health insurance policy you have a question about, the calendar of events from your local community center that you keep meaning to check out. It's crazy how an item weighing less than an ounce can require so much of your future time.

We understand that the tangible nature of paper has its benefits, that keeping a piece of paper is a physical reminder for you to complete a certain task. But what's important is understanding how much time those to-dos actually take. It's a matter of coming to terms with the amount of free time you actually have versus how much you think you have. A home piled with paperwork and unfinished projects is often the result of chronically underestimating how much time it will take to complete something. This reminds us of our client Maria.

Maria was a married mother of three children under the age of five. She ran her own successful graphic design consultancy and was an active board member of her community center. Her husband also worked full time and had an hour-long commute to work. On top of Maria's daily demands, there were always more e-mails, more obligations, more projects she had begun and not yet finished, more photos she wanted to get into albums, more cards she wanted to write to friends, and more family documents she needed to deal with on her parents' behalf. Maria, to put it lightly, had a lot on her plate.

We recognized that Maria suffered from something that is now so ingrained in many people's lives that they don't even see it anymore: the cycle of busyness. In our culture, the answer of "I'm so busy!" to the question of "How are you?" is respected, even revered. As a culture, we admire people who

cram as much as possible into their days, and it's worth noting how this correlates to the stuff filling our homes.

The overwhelming pressure of all the things we need to get done causes anxiety. Even in our moments of respite, we feel anxious because we are not in our accustomed state of busyness. The reflexive need to constantly be doing things to be productive is the type of behavior that prevents us from ever sitting down and reading that book or taking that leisurely walk in our neighborhood.

Segments of leisure, even boredom, are often described by social scientists and artists as the period in which magic happens. Leisure time is crucial. It gives us the chance to reflect upon our life and what we have learned, to create thoughtful responses to incoming information, and to chase curiosity and inspiration. To be fully present in your experiences, you need downtime. The thing to recognize is that no one is going to magically grant you leisure time. You need to carve it out and protect it. You have to end the cycle of busy for yourself. Say no to commitments of time and energy. Honor leisure time in the same way you honor other duties. As your world continues to ease up and slow down, you'll find that it becomes easier to say no and that leisure time will become a nonnegotiable part of your calendar.

For Maria and all her unfinished projects, we let the fact that they were simply that—unfinished—be the indicator that they were not her highest priority. We helped her figure out which were the essential projects and to-dos, and then she was able to let go of the rest. At this time in Maria's life, her top priorities were her kids' school-related commitments, her design firm, and her work at the community center. Any other project was subject to the chopping block, because extra projects are constant reminders of all the things you should be doing but aren't. That constant pressure to be doing something else is not good for your psyche, nor is it good for focusing on the task at hand. We encourage you to take this opportunity to wipe the slate clean and remove all those half-finished projects from your home, from your workspace, from your mind. Just imagine the feeling of freedom that will ensue.

DECLUTTERING
YOUR PAPERWORK

When sorting your paperwork, be ruthless about what you need to keep. You'll have five separate piles:

1 Archive—your most important documents, like birth certificates and social security cards

2 To-do (actual)—invitations to upcoming events, your child's field-trip form, a reminder that you are due for a smog check (select only those you actually need to do)

3 To-do (aspirational)—catalog of night classes, magazines, reviews for restaurants you'd like to try, free passes to a new gym, coupons to anything other than the grocery store (keep this pile lean and realistic)

4 Recycle—papers that you no longer need that don't have personal information on them

5 Shred—papers that you no longer need but that contain personal information

As you sort your paperwork, keep a running list of catalogs and mailings you need to unsubscribe from. At the end of the session, build in time to call or e-mail these establishments and request to be removed from their mailing lists. Save a few trees, and save yourself from the unneeded exposure to the temptation to buy more.

Moving forward in a more focused life, list making is a super important skill. When you start your day, write down your list of things to complete in the order of priority. And then adhere to that list. Cross things off as you go. And recycle the list at the end of the day. This is an especially important habit for readers who describe themselves as easily distracted.

TAKE ACTION: Tackle your junk mail once and for all. Part of the reason mail feels so daunting and builds up so quickly is the abundance of junk mail coming into our homes every day. Below are four simple steps to eliminate junk mail:

1 **Utilize Catalog Choice.** This amazing, free service (www .catalogchoice.org) allows you to create a profile for yourself (and any past residents of your home) in order to rapidly unsubscribe from catalogs and other mailings. (Pro tip: create profiles for "Current Resident" and "To Our Friends At" to stop those generic mailings as well.)

2 **Call them up.** There are some companies that Catalog Choice isn't able to help with unsubscribing from. For those companies, simply find their number on the back of the catalog, call them up, and ask to be removed from their mailings. When asked why we no longer wish to receive a company's catalog, we usually say something along the lines of "I do all of my shopping online and don't want to waste precious paper." The super sweet workers at L.L.Bean seemed to appreciate that.

3 **Fill out change-of-address forms for former residents at the post office.** If you happen to know the new address of your home's former resident, you can write it on the form. Otherwise you can write "no forwarding address." The good news is that change-of-address requests tend to be implemented rapidly (unlike catalogs, which can take six to eight weeks to stop being delivered).

4 **Get it by e-mail.** For documents that you still need to receive, sign up for electronic mailings instead. It takes a minute or two to create an online account, but it's worth it. You can often also sign up for automatic payments, ensuring that you never miss a bill in the future.

THE IMPORTANCE OF A LANDING ZONE

A vital piece to the puzzle of staying organized and sane is having a functional "landing zone" in the home. It is one area that we can safely say all homes require. We all shuttle in and out of our homes multiple times a day with objects like keys, wallets, phones, and sunglasses, yet so rarely is there a space in our homes dedicated to these most frequently used objects. What often happens instead is that these daily essential items are left scattered around the house on surfaces like the kitchen counter or the dining table. Typically, these items are placed in a rotating variety of locales depending on which surface is easiest to reach or least cluttered at any given moment, leading to the panicked last-minute search for the car keys when you are already running late.

To avoid that situation, it's crucial to create a landing zone for all those daily essentials. Kyle uses the following system: she puts her keys on one hook and her dog's leash on another, her jackets in the entryway closet, and her wallet, lip balm, and sunglasses in a tray on a shelf. Having a home for everything (yes, *everything* that currently lives at the bottom of your purse should have a home in the house) ensures that you never lose your things again. If you're the kind of person who enjoys switching out bags or purses, this is even more crucial for you.

It requires creating a ritual so that every time you enter your home—no matter how full your hands or how rushed you feel—you always take the time to put your things where they belong. The benefit is that no matter where you are headed or how tight your timeline is, you'll always be able to quickly grab exactly what you need as you head out the door.

HOBBIES, SPORTS + TOYS

———

Most-Affected Archetypes:
Energetic, Practical

Hobbies are one of the greatest joys in life. They are the things we pursue for pleasure, gratification, growth, and fulfillment. Whether this means an art, a craft, or a physical activity, for children and adults alike, our hobbies are a way to express ourselves with our bodies and our hearts. Yet just like with other categories of things, it is important to walk that middle path—to enjoy your leisure activities but not be owned by your hobbies.

One client in particular always comes to mind when we discuss hobbies. Carlos was a creative, energetic man in his forties, fresh out of a challenging divorce. He hired us to declutter and redesign his new home, which included a room devoted to music. When we arrived, we learned that the "music room" was more like a storage shed of all things music related. There were boxes of recording equipment stacked to the ceiling, taking up the majority of not just the floor space but all the inhabitable space in the room. We could barely walk through the ten-by-fourteen-foot room—there were rows of guitars and guitar stands, multiple keyboards, some stacked on top of each other, and two separate drum kits. On the surface, it appeared that Carlos was obsessed with the idea of having every possible instrument to record every possible sound.

We removed all the music equipment and staged it in a nearby room for decision making. As we helped Carlos sort, he told us that his ex-husband never allowed Carlos to have his music equipment on display or even realistically accessible in his former home. His instruments were confined to closets and strictly prohibited from being left out in the main areas of the home after he had used them.

Over time, Carlos naturally became more and more attached to the things that he wasn't allowed to have in his home. He started to habitually collect instruments, and his collection grew each time he felt his creativity being repressed. With the help of dear friends and a good therapist, Carlos uncovered that all this suppression of his passions made him feel as though he himself wasn't allowed to be in his own home.

This point of contention had played an integral part in splintering his marriage, and Carlos's feelings about it all came bubbling up during the decluttering process, making it difficult for him to let go of his music equipment. Since he'd never had the opportunity to freely interact with his instruments before, Carlos didn't know which ones he wanted to keep. All the instruments, even the duplicative ones, had their own special sounds and characteristics, and he had a hard time deciding which he would want to use in this new space.

It was clear that he had rigidly started to identify himself with his instruments—that donating his high school flute was like letting go of a piece of himself, denying himself the right to play the flute if he felt like it one day.

Over two slow, deliberate sessions, Carlos came to understand that in identifying himself with his things, his things were holding power over him. By separating his identity from his instruments, he was actually reasserting his power and control over his self-worth. Additionally, we helped him see that in practice, this method of collecting was not serving him—that being a jack-of-all-trades and keeping all these items made it difficult for him to actually use them, let alone master any.

Through our work we were able to hone in on Carlos's primary musical love—the guitar. He kept his favorite three guitars (one acoustic, a rare twelve-stringer, and one electric), his best amplifier, and one keyboard. That's it. In turn, his free time was no longer spent digging through piles of unused instruments to find the one he wanted to play. He was able to fit a desk in this room and even had space for a small couch from which he could watch movies on his large computer monitor. His dream of devoting a room to creative self-expression was finally realized.

DECLUTTERING YOUR HOBBIES, SPORTS + TOYS

When you declutter items related to your hobbies, sports equipment, and craft supplies, it's not so much about how to physically execute the decluttering as it is about answering questions such as the following:

— How much free time do I actually have, and what do I most want to do with it?

— Am I allowing myself to progress and grow in areas that matter to me?

— Do the hobbies, sports equipment, or toys in my home reflect my current interests?

There is only so much physical space in any of our homes, and we are all limited to the same twenty-four-hour day. It's great to evolve, to continue to unfold. Following your curiosity will allow you to be creative in ways that a room packed full with craft supplies will not. Think about it this way: are you done with

your scrapbooking phase, and do you now enjoy editing digital videos? Awesome! Embrace and make space for that new hobby by letting go of the tools from your old one. Conversely, if you are devoted to a single hobby, let go of any need to diversify. Become an expert at that one thing. For as long as it inspires you, embrace it.

Cary often thinks about this as it applies to her own life. Limiting their number of hobbies was perhaps the first way in which she and Cam went minimalist, not out of an elevated attempt at mindfulness but out of necessity. When they first started dating, they each had a vast array of hobbies, which they pursued at random throughout the course of any given week. In trying to spend time together, they found that they needed to develop new criteria for co-recreation: they both needed to enjoy the activity, and they needed to be at a similar enough skill level that they would enjoy doing that activity together. The one activity that fit this criteria was a deep love for hiking and trail running.

As Cary and Cam both grew busier and had conflicting schedules, an unspoken rule emerged: on their rare overlapping free days together, they would find a trail to run. They loved to wake up, get dressed, and be on their way with no drama. They found variety by choosing from dozens of trails of varying lengths and degrees of difficulty. They had the option to bring a picnic lunch or a hammock and book. Maybe their route would take them to a lake or a stream or the ocean for a dip. They still had so many options, but the gear and the decisions were simple, which meant that Cary and Cam got to use their free time in the way that was most important to them: together, in nature. Even after their schedules were aligned once again, they found such clarity and creativity in their hiking routine that they still stick to this plan every weekend. This simple routine shows up in the house as well, for it allowed them to donate all their extra-specialized gear, balls, and bikes.

WHAT'S YOUR KRYPTONITE?

What situation is your personal Kryptonite, your weak spot when it comes to stuff? What store do you always come out of with more than you intended to buy? Is it hard for you to resist the deals when there's an online flash sale? Do you have a hard time saying no to things, like the freebies given out at work? Do you end up going shopping with friends even when you don't need anything? Taking the time to understand the scenarios in which you end up buying things just because it feels good is imperative to changing your consumption habits. Once you understand that those feel-good moments you get from acquiring things are fleeting (and furthermore require the acquisition of more and more things to continue the high), you will be one up on the habitual buying patterns so many of us engage in without a second thought. Before you enter your Kryptonite store, be armed with a list of what you need.

The easiest way to reduce clutter in the long term is to stop it before it ever enters your house. As soon as something enters your home, it is automatically more difficult to say no to this thing, because you've already said yes to it. Ask yourself, "Why am I bringing these items across my threshold in the first place?" and listen closely for the answer. This will save untold money, time, and energy in the future!

SENTIMENTAL ITEMS + KEEPSAKES

Most-Affected Archetype: Connected

Over the past year, up until writing this book, Cary had been treading through the decluttering land mine of sentimental childhood keepsakes. Her parents had decided to downsize and move out of her childhood home. This meant that all her photos, art projects, writing, diaries, awards, and other artifacts of growing up (which until this point had been conveniently stored in her parents' basement) were suddenly hers to deal with.

Arriving at Cary's San Francisco apartment inside of a cardboard box and a large suitcase were memories from every part of her life, from birth until she moved to California at twenty-four years old. Every sports ribbon she'd earned, every photo she'd ever taken, even her first pair of shoes—it was all there.

When Cary opened these boxes, she felt as if everything inside them was a treasure, a marker of a time in her life that could never be re-created. Each object or written page felt like a crucial piece in the puzzle of who she was. Not only that, but everything had been kept for so long already. These keepsakes had been stored for decades in Illinois and then lovingly boxed up and brought to California by her mom. Obviously, everything would have to stay. Or would it?

It all relates to the psychological hypothesis of the endowment effect, which maintains that the longer we've had something in our possession, the more value it holds in our eyes. Combine this feeling with a healthy dose of nostalgia, and suddenly it seems unfathomable to part with a single piece of artwork from kindergarten. In an attempt to match her actions with her words (that is, to try not to be a total sham of a minimalist), Cary decided to question everything and sort each item, one by one.

On the surface, each item was of somewhat equal merit: it was from her past and had, at some point, been deemed worthy of saving. So to help her through this process, she called on Canadian entrepreneur Danielle LaPorte's wisest advice: to pay attention exclusively to how each item made her feel. And while every object was tinged with a bit of nostalgia, some created a real sense of happiness (keep) and others fell flat or unearthed feelings of sadness, resentment, or embarrassment (let go).

Somehow, even after this paring down, Cary still felt ill at ease. She'd attempted to integrate her memorabilia throughout her home (what good are memories if they are stored in boxes?) but instead of making her feel rooted and joyful, she felt out of balance. It was as though her brain were a radio stuck between two frequencies. On her walls were items that constantly pulled her into the past, while her current life was still occurring around her, without her full attention.

Is not the best way for us to honor our past—the people and experiences and heartbreak and deepest joys that made us who we are—to be fully present? To create space for our future to unfold? The deepest way to honor your past is to honor your current self, to love and cherish those around you, and to know all those experiences from your past are inherently a part of you, whether or not a photo of them resides on your wall.

So Cary opted to do one more deep purge of her childhood keepsakes. Her most beloved photos now live in one scrapbook. Her most treasured writings and artwork live in a small folder. Since these items are so easily accessible now, she can pull out photos of her childhood best friend at a moment's notice to celebrate her birthday or open up her younger self's diary from camp when she needs a sense of perspective. Yet the ease with which she can access these memories also denotes how easily she can tuck them away—with a single hand—and enjoy her life in the present.

HERE'S THE THING ABOUT COLLECTIONS

Do you have someone in your life who is an avid collector? Does your grandmother have, for example, a collection of crystal animal figurines? How did that collection start? Perhaps it began as a phase in her thirties, when she traveled to France and found her first crystal teddy bear. And then the teddy bear garnered a crystal alligator friend in Florida. Soon, Grandma had a nice collection of crystal animals representing all her travels, displayed on her bookcase at home. Of course, other people then took notice, and soon enough, family members and friends decided to bring her crystal animals from *their* travels.

Now all available surfaces in Grandma's house are covered with crystal animal figurines. Anyone who enters Grandma's house knows right away that she is a collector of small crystal animal figurines. At age eighty-five, she spends her precious time and energy dusting them and worrying about keeping them safe and who will take care of them when she's gone. This scenario illustrates just how easy it is for collections to take on a life of their own.

Why is it that we feel the desire to collect in the first place? What do we believe our collections say about us? If you feel as though part of your identity is inextricably connected to the items that you own, this might be an example of your things having too much power over you. Because if your identity and self-worth are connected to material things, you are tethering your happiness to something outside of yourself. Meaning that your happiness is dependent on outside conditions, conditions that can and will fluctuate throughout your life. Knowing the true reason behind your desire to collect is a powerful way to exert your authority over your things.

So how do you keep your collection in check? Select a reasonably sized container to hold all parts of your collection. Once the collection outgrows its container, you know it's time to select your favorites and let go of the rest. Don't allow the objects you don't enjoy a free pass just because they're part of a larger group. The more selective you are about your items, the more each will shine and get the attention it deserves.

DECLUTTERING YOUR SENTIMENTAL ITEMS

Keepsakes and sentimental items make up the category that deserves your most present and relaxed self for sorting; be certain to refer back to the section on your archetype's tools. It's unavoidable—and thus should be both expected and accepted with grace—that objects from your past will stir up a variety of emotions, some of which can be quite challenging. Take the time before sorting to ask yourself the crucial questions: "How do I want to feel?" and "Does this item make me feel that way?"

This is not to say that we need to ignore hard times in our lives and that anything that's even a little negative needs to go. If that were the case, we would all have to toss out photos from those awkward teenage years with questionable fashion choices. But there is power in deciding what narrative you want to tell about your own life. Adolescence is kind to few. Bad past girlfriends or boyfriends abound, and braces look good on no one. Those experiences all played a role in shaping the people we are today. But not all life phases or experiences from our past need to be continually invited into our present.

Think about it this way. Did you ever have a challenging friend or teacher or bully growing up? Is it still a little tender to think about? Did you learn something from the situation, even if it took years of distance and maybe a little therapy? Then give yourself permission to bless and release the physical reminders from that time. Not every part of your past is equally worth holding on to, and the most important part of your life is currently unfolding.

So take the time to look at each photo, each essay, each snow globe. Thank each item for having been a part of your history, for contributing to making you the person you are today. And then be highly selective about the items that you choose to keep around and bring with you into the future. These items will make you feel the way you want to feel, tell a crucial part of your life story, and fit into containers, scrapbooks, or photo albums that are easy to access and put away.

TAKE ACTION: Give gifts that don't add to the clutter. Over the holidays, at birthday parties, and at wedding and baby showers, we want to show the people in our lives that we care, but how can we do it without buying a bunch of things? These five gift ideas are not only earth friendly and easy on the budget, they are also just downright thoughtful.

- **Play travel agent.** Go beyond the normal gift-certificate idea, and plan an activity for your friend or family member instead. Get into the details. Plan a picnic where you bring the supplies, and select the spot. Or go for something simple like a round of drinks at your favorite watering hole. The key here is to be specific. Kyle once gifted a "day o' fun" for a friend's wedding. It included tickets to an all-day music festival in the wine country. She took care of all the details and made sure that the newlyweds reserved the date. What a wonderful luxury it was for them to spend an entire day together.

- **Make something yummy.** It doesn't have to be your regular old apple pie (unless that's your thing . . . in which case, do it!). Out-of-the-box ideas include creating a custom tea blend and packaging it in little tins or making your favorite salad dressing and putting it in reusable glass jars. Or for your friend who is hosting a holiday party, offer to make (beforehand) a special mixer for a festive cocktail! The yummy possibilities are endless . . .

- **Handwrite a letter.** Sit down and write a letter explaining all the ways in which you love that person. Write a rough draft first, and then transfer it to the real card. We pretty much type on keyboards all the time now, so this gives you an opportunity to brush up on your handwriting skills. For extra credit, enlist the help of friends to create a collection of love letters for a special occasion!

- **Give a speech.** For the holidays, Cary and her family have the sweetest ritual. With three siblings and two parents, it would be a lot of gift giving if everyone had to buy gifts for each other. Instead, every year they draw names, and then each of them writes a speech about his or her assigned family member. They have several weeks to think about and write the speech. On Christmas day, they recite their speech and rejoice in each other's attributes. What was once a financial burden and stressful chore has been turned into a celebration of each other. How wonderful is that?

- **Give to a charity.** Make a donation to an organization that the giftee is passionate about. Thinking hard about a charity that will actually resonate with the person shows that you really know them and care about their interests.

- **And finally,** when it comes time to wrap your gifts, bear in mind that holiday-specific gift wrap can easily multiply and take up tons of space in your home. Instead, buy one roll of brown construction paper that can be used for any occasion, and decorate the gift yourself (using fun magazine and news-paper photos, doodling a pattern with a Sharpie, or making potato stamps to personalize your wrapping paper). Kids can even get into the fun when gift wrapping becomes a craft in and of itself.

DECOR + FURNITURE

Most-Affected Archetype:
Frugal, Connected

The thing that perhaps all our clients have in common is that we have yet to advise anyone at the end of a session to go out and buy a bunch of decor. Cary can't even imagine Kyle saying something like "Go make a Target run, pick up a bunch of mirrored boxes, and find some random object in green to tie this space together." Items acquired from the "home decor" section of any big-box store lack character. They are inherently mass produced or at least mass consumed, and surrounding yourself with items like these is less than inspiring. Rapidly acquiring decor to outfit your entire home also means that each item will remind you of an exact, narrow moment of time in your life. We advocate decor that is intentionally acquired over time and through life's layers of experiences to bring variety and visual interest to a space. Use decor to reflect your intentions, hopes, and imagination. Many of our clients have functional items that they love, like instruments, plants, jewelry, or lighting, that add worlds of character to a space and can dually serve as decor.

One client we recall fondly when discussing this topic is a vibrant young professional in San Francisco named Rebekah. She was dealing with something so common for people in their twenties: she was renting out a simple room in a shared flat. This meant that everything she owned had to find a home in her one little room with meager closet space. It further meant that this space was impermanent; she didn't want to take the time to buy items specifically for it, and her landlord forbade her to paint the walls. As a result, her room felt overrun by stuff (athletic gear, work clothes, and camping gear) while simultaneously feeling empty due to her blank walls.

Before delving into decluttering her space, we asked her about her style: which of her possessions was she most attracted to? Downcast, Rebekah said she felt utterly directionless, unclear on any type of style when it came to adorning her room. She claimed that decorating simply wasn't a talent that she possessed. This was early in our days working together as New Minimalism.

We took her word that she wasn't stylistically inclined and told her we'd help her come up with a decorating strategy after our decluttering session.

Then, after a deep purging, we ended up with some unexpected items that worked as the most gorgeous decor: her banjo was mounted to the wall, her favorite vinyl albums were propped up in her bookcase, her rug—which had been folded and collecting dust under her bed—was now proudly hung from the wall in place of a headboard, and a lamp that her father had made was given a place of honor.

Not a single one of these items was new or borrowed from the common spaces. All these items were ones she had picked out with care; she loved them already. The objects, given the space and the attention they deserved, absolutely shined. And Rebekah simply radiated joy the moment she stepped into a room that reflected and supported her core self. All three of us, Kyle, Cary, and Rebekah, learned a powerful lesson that day: everyone does have a sense of style; sometimes it just needs to be rediscovered and dusted off!

DECLUTTERING
DECOR

So you've decluttered your wardrobe, kitchen, household supplies, home office, hobbies, and keepsakes—basically all the smaller items in your home. Now it's time to tackle home decor (we will get to furniture shortly). This means removing all the paintings and other artwork from the walls and gathering all the candlesticks and other items on display. You may have tackled some of these items in your keepsakes round. Now it's time to address everything else. It is helpful to pull out seasonal decorations, too.

Just like you did with your wardrobe, pull out your five favorite decor items and look at them closely. Consider the unifying elements they have in common. A similar color scheme might emerge. Or you might find that you love natural materials like clay and leather. Or that you prefer shiny metals paired with bright colors. We had one client who described her style as modern and sleek, but when we came to her home and she picked out her favorite things, we realized she actually loved more traditional Asian decoration set against a clean white backdrop. So take this time to let your favorite items speak for themselves. When decorating your redesigned space, be sure to give your favorite items center stage in the design.

DECLUTTERING
FURNITURE

When considering your furniture, play around with the arrangement. Now that you have fewer things in your home, it should be easier to move furniture around to find the ideal layout. Remember the primary function you've declared for each room, and make sure that the furniture supports that. This is the time to reimagine and play. What if you didn't have a coffee table so that it was easier to practice yoga or play with your kids on a whim? What if you used a small rug to define a reading nook in your living room? Physically play with new arrangements, even if it's just to confirm a bad idea so you won't be left to wonder, "What if?" It took three different tries to conclude that Kyle's couch worked best at an angle in the middle of the living room, facing the fireplace—not something she could have guessed without trying it first.

CHAPTER 7

The Design Principles

Now that you've decluttered your home, it's time to put it back together beautifully. Traditionally, interior decorating focuses on *adding* elements to the equation in order to enhance an interior. And we are here to dispel that misconception. Over the years we have developed the following twelve design principles as ways to improve your space without buying anything new.

The design principles work across all varieties of homes to help create a clutter-free sanctuary. Whether you live in a suburban single-family home or in a downtown city loft, whether your style is boho or modern, these principles work because they focus on overall systems and philosophies rather than specifying the exact types of things you should or should not have.

Furthermore, these principles address the questions that continually surface during our client sessions. By explaining these principles in detail, we can ensure that we are all operating from the same frame of reference as we put a space back together. We hope they'll help guide your decisions when redesigning your interiors.

Design Principle #1: Redefine your definition of *full*.

This design principle (perhaps our favorite) was born of an epiphany we had after a long wardrobe-decluttering day with clients. At the end of the session, we gave the couple a tour of their newly decluttered master bedroom. When we arrived at a (previously stuffed-to-the-brim) sock drawer, we noted how all the socks were clearly visible, making it quick to grab the desired pair, and how the drawer opened and closed with ease. Just before moving on to the next drawer, Kyle stated, somewhat off the cuff, "So consider this drawer as being full."

Our client's eyes opened wide, and she said, "Really? Wow, I see. This is full. I get it now." We realized that up to that point we had taken for granted that we all shared a definition of *full*, when in fact New Minimalism was defining *full* differently than the average person—especially our lovely clients, who had enlisted our help to deal with their clutter. At every session since then, we have made sure to define *full*.

We always default to the simplest solution, and our definition of *full* is no exception. For New Minimalism, *full* means that the items within the confines of the drawer, cabinet, or closet have ample space to be seen and can be accessed with ease.

A space is *too* full when:

- Items are piled so high that it is difficult to access the items at the bottom without toppling everything over
- Items are stacked so deep that you can no longer see what is at the back of the drawer, cabinet, or closet
- You cannot open or close a drawer, cabinet, or closet with one hand, because you are using the other hand to stuff down the contents that are spilling out the top or over the side

This photo of cooking pans is a great example of our definition of full. The pans are arranged in such a way that they are easy to grab and easy to put away. Yes, the drawer could physically fit more items inside, but adding more to this drawer would make it cumbersome to access all the contents.

Design Principle #2: Put your dresser in your closet.

OK, to be fair, not everyone needs a dresser per se, but everyone needs some version of drawers or bins for small wardrobe items like underwear, socks, scarves, winter hats, and swimsuits. Dressers are what we tend to use in the United States, and they work beautifully for these exact items. Plus, the sturdiness and character of a well-made wooden dresser and the warmth and texture it adds to a space are a nice bonus.

So let's say your bedroom contains a decent-sized closet plus a freestanding dresser. Imagine all the square footage you would gain if you were able to combine the dresser and closet into one. Use this as a goal in your decluttering, the signal of a successful paring down. If the infrastructure of your closet allows, you can simply slide your freestanding dresser into your closet. If you have fixed, built-in wooden shelves inside your closet, you could instead buy clothing-friendly baskets to be placed on the shelves, essentially mimicking drawers, and get rid of your dresser.

DESIGNING YOUR OWN BUILT-IN CLOSET SYSTEM

If your closet has only hanging rods and a dresser won't fit inside, consider the worthy investment of a built-in closet system. We have worked with many different closet systems, and we recommend using Elfa, a modular system that offers a variety of designs and is made of durable materials.

The recommended order of operations: first thoroughly declutter your wardrobe, then design your ideal closet system. Most closet systems require you to order through a trained closet/design specialist. It will be much easier to explain your desired design to the closet specialist once you know exactly how much space you need for each subcategory of your wardrobe (e.g., space for long-hanging garments versus space for short-hanging garments). Just know that when you enlist the help of a specialist to design the configuration of your custom closet system, these

(left) We used a dresser to remedy the lack of shelving in this closet, making the lower half of the space more functional.

specialists, with the best intentions, are trained to maximize your space and add in all the little doodads that you "need" to most efficiently store all your things (for example, a pull-out tie holder with fifty-plus notches for your fifty-plus ties). When we designed this closet system, we found out that we needed only six drawers, although there was space for eight. Design your space for only what is needed, and then leave extra space between each drawer, allowing the contents to be simply stored and easily accessed.

BEFORE

AFTER

Design Principle #3:
Use existing storage
before adding more.

Unless you live in a drastically atypical space, you probably have at least one closet in your home and some cabinets in the kitchen. So let's start here, with the storage you do have.

We say that New Minimalism is partly a Zen practice because we focus each session on what is, not what might be. In other words, we work with the space as it exists in this moment. Rather than imagining how a longed-for space or furniture item might be, we use the existing closet space, furniture, and decor before recommending that our client add anything new. Paired with focused problem solving and a little imagination, we often find that at the end of the day our clients rarely need to bring in additional items to enhance the space. The clients who come to us saying that they need to tear out all their closets and build new ones often need only a strategically placed shelf divider or hooks installed to remedy the situation.

By approaching the design of your space with this principle in mind, you may find creative ways to use the space that you missed before. Make sure you take the time to look at your space with fresh eyes. Lastly, never underestimate the use of baskets, trays, small bins, and other containers you come across in your decluttering. Set these items aside for the time being, and see whether you can use them to enhance the existing storage of your space when you put everything back.

TAKE ACTION: Buy bulk. Seeking out food from the bulk containers is one of the best ways to reduce the amount of trash you produce. Most groceries will have at least a modest bulk section. In the Bay Area we are lucky to have an abundance of bulk-friendly grocery stores: Rainbow Grocery (San Francisco), Berkeley Bowl (Berkeley), and Good Earth Natural Foods (Fairfax). Another great option, as Cary discovered in Boise, is to find and join a local co-op. It's a great community to be a part of, and most co-ops have extensive bulk sections (the Boise co-op has three types of miso paste in bulk). In some European cities, there are grocery stores that are 100 percent packaging-free, like Original Unverpackt in Berlin. Be a champion for zero waste when it comes to packaging, and support the bulk bins!

Tips for buying bulk:

- Most stores that provide bulk bins also sell reusable glass jars and cotton bags to transport your bulk items. If cotton bags are not an option, use small paper or compostable bags before reaching for single-use plastic bags.
- *Tare weight* is the weight of an empty container. When you bring your own glass or plastic container to use in the bulk section, you'll need to have the tare weight measured before

you fill your container. Stores with large bulk sections usually have an assistant available to help you with this.

- Rather than writing the food ID number on those twist ties, use a notepad or an application on your phone. You'll just have to pay attention during checkout and tell the cashier what is what. Or if you use paper bags, you can write directly on the paper.
- Know the size of your containers at home so that you don't accidentally buy twice as much as you can properly store.
- Linger in the bulk aisle and see what catches your eye. You may be surprised by what you find.

TAKE ACTION: Do you like the *idea* of composting but actually hate it in practice? This is probably because old food starts to stink, and taking out the compost on a daily basis is just not happening. Here is our solution: store it in the freezer! Yes, that means you have to make room in your freezer to hold your food scraps. But by freezing them, you remove the smell factor, so you don't have to take out your compost until your freezer bin is full.

Kyle prefers to use a brown paper bag with the top cut down to fit in her freezer. She then composts the entire bag once it is full. Cary prefers to use the plastic bins in which she occasionally purchases her spinach. Once the bin is full, she dumps the compost. And after several uses she recycles the plastic bin. Our friend Hannah uses the plastic storage bin that came in her freezer (for ice storage) and a compostable bag liner. If your city provides municipal composting services, it simply couldn't be easier! If you're like Cary, who doesn't have access to such services in Boise, see our Resources section for several simple, easy ways to start your own composting system at home.

Design Principle #4: Sometimes, the best use of a space is to leave it empty.

This principle is considered advanced, because it goes one step further than Design Principle #3, which asks you to utilize your home's current storage options. This principle challenges you to understand which areas in your home are a pain to access, and then to choose to leave those spaces empty. That attic that requires a death-defying ladder routine, that closet that is so narrow and long only your cat can get to the back of it, that top shelf where you put just-in-case gifts (which is also the shelf that you can't see very well and therefore always forget to give the gifts at the time of the event)—these are all examples of hard-to-reach or inaccessible places that are better left unused. We have even coined a name for it: dead space. Save yourself the

headache of tossing something there that you can never retrieve and just pretend these spaces don't exist.

One indicator that you have indeed completed a thorough and sweeping decluttering of your home is that you no longer have a need for those deep, dark, spider-ridden areas. When you whittle down your possessions to only the essentials, it becomes easy to leave the attic clear of guest bedding, because all your bedding fits in the linen closet. You no longer use that hard-to-reach shelf to store your five backup bottles of body lotion, because those bottles are long gone.

FRESH AIR

An easy way to improve air quality in your home, assuming you don't live next to a freeway overpass (like Kyle did back in her Brooklyn days), is to crack the window to circulate fresh air. Another way is to bring in some plants—houseplants bring life to your interiors and improve air quality. We would argue that the houseplant trend is here to stay, and for good reason!

Design Principle #5: Find a home for everything.

(bottom right) Here, you can see that all the pens live in a mug on the desk. If you ever need a pen, you go to this mug. If a pen is on the table and you are getting ready for dinner, it goes back to its home in the mug with its other pen friends. Easy-peasy.

"A place for everything and everything in its place." This phrase is often cited in the boating world because on a boat, space is at such a premium that everything needs its specific place. If you happened to need a certain tool in an emergency, for example, and it wasn't where it was meant to be, a situation could quickly become dangerous. Even in a less serious situation, in such tight quarters even a few things out of place can make the entire vessel unravel into chaos. In the same way, regardless of your home's size, we believe that all items in your house should live in a specific place.

One of the biggest benefits of living this way is that you quickly know when items are out of place. Tidying up takes more effort when you are not sure where you should place the items that have collected on surfaces and are stacked in corners. On the other hand, we tell clients that if every item has a clear, fitting home, it actually becomes harder to leave things out of place rather than to simply put them where they belong. The main goal, therefore, is for all items to have such a clearly defined home that it would take active effort to leave things out of place and messy.

As you begin to put each space back together after decluttering, find a permanent home for each item with plenty of room for it to be accessed and appreciated.

TAKE ACTION: Deal with your mail! One of the most obvious yet elusive habits we've seen missing in otherwise highly effective adults is dealing with mail. We've seen clients with drawers and paper bags and under-the-bed bins (talk about bad feng shui) full of unopened mail. And while 99 percent of that mail might be offers for credit cards you don't want, the truth is that unopened mail weighs heavy on our subconscious. There's likely a bill (or a check!) or something else important that you need to tend to in that stack.

If you suffer from a major mail pileup, rather than continuing to ignore it, set a timer for forty-five minutes to quickly tackle as much mail as possible. Don't defer this task any longer. Before starting, set up a recycling bin and a "to-shred" bag, then tear through your mail. In the end you will likely be left with a small pile of to-dos, yet they will all be *known* to-dos, which are so much easier on our brains. Moving forward, make sure that as soon as you get your mail from your box or front door, you open all important pieces, then shred and recycle them once they are no longer needed. If you don't have time to open your mail, we would recommend leaving it in the mailbox until you do have time, rather than bringing it in and not sorting it. Otherwise piles will start to grow.

Design Principle #6: Use boundaries to indicate when a category is full.

Using boundaries to indicate when a category is "full" is a universally applicable principle. It is effective in all homes and useful in every category. Once you declutter your scarves and determine how many you need, you can find the appropriately sized basket to hold them. If in a few months you are gifted two new scarves and then scarves are spilling out over the top of the basket, your container is telling you, "Hey, it's time to declutter your scarves again!"

This principle holds especially true for hobbies and sports equipment. If you love to ride bikes and have a habit of holding on to spare parts in case they may come in handy one day, give yourself some boundaries. Use a small box to hold your tools and spare parts, and whenever the parts begin to exceed their boundaries, it's time to take a trip to the bike shop and see whether the people there have a use for those extra pedals or that handlebar tape.

One of the best things about young children is that they work especially well when given boundaries for their things. As the parent, you get to decide when there is too much of something, and we encourage you to use physical boundaries to teach your children this principle. As you can see in the photo on page 162, you can use simple wicker baskets and easy-to-read labels to indicate which toys go where. If the toy collection grows and overtakes its given boundaries, then it is time to prune the collection and give the unused toys to children in need in your community.

Regardless of whether the items are related to your hobby of knitting, your penchant for outdoor adventures, or your love of building electronics, we encourage you to set up boundaries to limit the space these items take up. These items are often part of projects you are passionate about, so it is even more crucial to create boundaries for them so that you do not get carried away and all of a sudden find that you have an entire room devoted to needlepoint, your fifth-favorite hobby. Marie Kondo had it right when she wrote, "Human beings can only truly cherish a limited number of things at one time."

Design Principle #7: Remove electronics from the bedroom.

While electronics like cell phones, tablets, or laptops might be necessities for work, in our downtime, particularly as we transition to sleep and waking, we need to take caution.

Electronic toys, with their illuminated screens, stimulate the brain. More and more research confirms that "the spectrum of light emitted from your cell phone screen triggers your brain to secrete more 'daytime hormones,' which delays and reduces the secretion of the sleepy-time hormone melatonin." In other words, electronics keep you awake. Furthermore, this hormone disruption muddles your REM sleep patterns, decreasing the quality of your sleep, which might explain your feeling groggy in the morning, even after several hours of sleep.

Equally as important as getting ready for bed is the way in which you start your day. For the love of all things sane and good, please do not wake up and immediately check your cell phone! This puts you in a reactive, urgent headspace. First

things first, be sure to check in with yourself and prioritize your own goals for the day before allowing other people's concerns and desires in. There is a reason for the current popularity of cultivating a morning routine.

Your bedroom is a *bed*room, not an office room, nor a media room, nor a breakfast nook. Ideally it radiates calm and peacefulness. Imagine a gorgeous health and wellness spa where every detail, from the scent to the fabrics to the art on the wall, is geared toward aiding relaxation. Use that as inspiration for your bedroom!

Like all items in your home, electronics, when not in use, need a specific place to live. We suggest creating a charging station in a centralized area where phones and tablets can be placed when they are not in use. A perfect place for the charging station is near the front door, in the home office, or in another area where active, daytime behavior occurs in the house. Enforce a house rule of refraining from checking your phone or e-mail in the hour leading up to bedtime. In addition to increasing the time between screen time and sleep, there are phone settings and apps you can set to emit less stimulating blue light and more yawn-inducing red light during the evening (so graphic designers, do your color-specific work during the daytime hours). All these tricks will help corral your electronic toys into an active area of the home, reserving your bedroom for all things bedroom related.

Design Principle #8: Allow one to stand for many.

At their best, our homes are a reflection of our hopes, our current values, and our history. While having meaningful objects from our pasts can be beautiful, we need to achieve a fine balance, lest we become rooted in our history and unable to move forward into our future. Karen Kingston, an expert on decluttering, states it best: "When you are surrounded by more than 50 percent of belongings that remind you of something from your past, you will continue to live in the past." It is difficult to boldly pave your way forward when you are clouded by memories and nostalgia.

One way to keep things from your past from holding such power over you is to allow one object to stand for many. Let us explain: if you consider yourself a world traveler, use your finest piece of art from all your travels to represent your entire travel career. If travel really is a value of yours, then we will assume that you are traveling quite frequently. It would be a challenge to have to keep a memento from every trip you have ever taken. Relieve yourself of that self-imposed burden and instead choose what item will represent the whole.

Kyle, for example, has one beautiful black-and-white photograph of her grandmother. This is the only family photo that is displayed in her home. And while she has a collection of other cherished family photos in a box of mementos, she chooses

to display only this one image. She is thankful for the close relationship she has with her parents and brother, but she doesn't feel that every family member needs to be displayed to show her love for them. The one lovely image of her mother's mother is enough to remind her of the importance of her family and personal history.

Design Principle #9: Use blank space to elevate objects.

Much as an art gallery or museum leaves plenty of white space around each piece, you can do the same with functional, everyday pieces from your own life to elevate them to the level of art. Leaving blank space around an object bestows a sense of reverence and visual importance to that object—no matter how quotidian or functional it is. Hang a beaded necklace in the center of a wall, and the surrounding wall becomes its frame. The subtle textures of a hand-thrown artisan vase are explicitly noticeable when it stands on a table all by itself.

ODD NUMBERS

It's a classic design trick—odd-numbered groupings of objects look best together. When there is an odd number, the eye can quickly deduce that a focal point exists. With an even grouping, the objects become blurry and confusing.

Design Principle #10: Buy secondhand for a unique home.

"Style has absolutely nothing to do with money" is the matter-of-fact advice from UK decorator Abigail Ahern (*Decorating with Style*). If you value having a home that is unique to you and your experiences, become adept at shopping your local secondhand stores. Yes, it requires a little gumption, perseverance, and patience, but this is the number-one way to have a home that is unique and true to your own style. Have you ever walked into a home and noted that all the furniture was from the same designer and the same collection? It kind of feels as though you accidentally stumbled into a Pottery Barn or West Elm catalog. Even if the furniture technically goes together, it's obviously missing soul and distinction. The home could belong to anyone who has access to a credit card and a catalog. In other words, boring!

The Internet is a beautiful thing and is not to be discounted as an excellent resource. As long as Craigslist is around, we will be using it to recommend furniture for clients. Use keywords in your search if you have a specific style in mind, or keep it totally open. You never know what you might find, what might inspire you.

People move across the country at the drop of a hat nowadays. Seek out those people who are off-loading perfectly great furniture because they can't take it with them. This is also the best way to find quality items for half the price. On a decorating job in Los Angeles, Kyle found an amazing vintage dining table and four chairs for $900. It was much better quality and cheaper than something she would have found at a store, and it is now unique to that client's home. Cary's entire first bedroom in San Francisco was courtesy of a woman moving to New York. For $400 she got a double-wide dresser and two bedside tables, not to mention a mirror and dishes thrown in for free!

TAKE ACTION: If you do choose to buy new, it is important to put your hard-earned dollars toward supporting what you believe in. Materials and sourcing matter. Read tags and ask questions. With manufacturing and sourcing practices becoming more and more transparent, the answers to these questions should be readily available.

Design Principle #11: Use task lighting for immediate ambiance.

If you rent an apartment that suffers from terrible lighting, we have some good news: lamps, lamps, lamps! Task lighting refers to any lighting source that is used for specific tasks, like a reading lamp on your desk or under-cabinet lights for your kitchen counters. Overhead lights can be harsh and overbearing, so rather than rely on them for your lighting needs, invest in a lamp or two. Get unconventional and use a decorative lamp in your kitchen. A little party trick: don't forget about the little light in the hood of your oven. This can provide instant mood lighting for your dinner party. Much like candlelight, lamplight immediately ups the cozy factor and creates ambiance by softening visual edges.

One summer, Kyle spent a week in Copenhagen. With her penchant for beautiful interior lighting, Kyle was in heaven in Copenhagen. Accustomed to long winter nights, the Danes know a thing or two about the value of good lighting. Even the dive bars have beautiful vintage pendants strung from the ceiling, illuminating nooks and crannies where one can hole up with a friend to share a conversation. Plus, they have a strong candle culture—nearly every apartment window displays a beautiful candelabra. What surprised Kyle the most was how the Danes had an irreverence for the electrical cords that made the lighting possible. Rather than deal with the expense of hardwiring a sconce or pendant, they just pinned the cord (also called the "swag") aside or let several cords dangle together, as if they were an art piece. It was refreshing to see lighting design that wasn't restricted by the need to hide cords and hardwire it into the wall.

Embrace lighting as the Danes do, and don't let a visible electrical cord thwart your lighting goals. This carefree approach opens up a whole world of lighting opportunities.

Design Principle #12:
Let your freak flag
fly, while leaving
space for others.

We love when clients have confidence in their specific tastes and pride in their personal style. Variety makes life more interesting. And while we condone standing tall in your design preferences, we understand that there is still a balance to maintain, especially if you share a home, rent your home to guests, or aspire to share a home with someone.

Imagine you just started dating someone, and you arrive at his or her house for the first time to see that it is chock-full of personal mementos and possessions. The closet is brimming with clothes, and the bathroom barely has any free space to put a guest toothbrush. The refrigerator door is crammed with photos, cards, and ticket stubs. Subconsciously you might feel that people who live in such spaces are signaling that there is no room for you, that they are content filling their space with just their things and do not need nor desire to share it with anyone else. If this is the message you want to send, then continue to keep a space like the one we just described. But if you share a home or are looking to share a space in the future, be mindful of how full your home is. We don't need to know *everything* about you just by looking around your home. Drop hints, yes, but refrain from displaying your life's entire glorious history in the form of tchotchkes.

When you walk into a space for the first time, notice what, if anything, makes you feel comfortable and relaxed. Is it the lighting or the ability to sit on the couch without having to first remove catalogs and clothing? Is it a hook for your jacket and a place to rest your bag? Then notice what makes you feel nervous to move or touch anything for fear of messing it up. Is it that everything is too perfectly placed? Or is the space so full that you are afraid you might knock something over? The differences between a welcoming space and an overbearing space might simply be the number of things in the space. As you decorate your own home, let your freak flag fly, but at the same time, leave some space for others to feel comfortable, too.

AFTERWORD

The intention of this entire process of decluttering and redesign-ing your home is to streamline the basics of your life so that you have the energy, space, and clarity to focus your life force on what matters most to you. Throughout this book, we've noted that when your space is crazy, it's often because you are feeling scattered, overwhelmed, and so on.

Our tagline at New Minimalism has long been this message: *Your external space reflects your internal state. What does your home say about you?*

This is our favorite question to ask because it presupposes that our homes and our minds are connected, that the two are linked and in continuous conversation with one another. When we see our clients' homes in total disarray, they almost always tell us, "I feel overwhelmed. I don't even know where to begin."

Energetically and visually, our spaces tend to reflect our men-tal states. Yet the converse is also often true. Our homes impact and shape how we feel. Even those of us who are good at com-partmentalizing (we're looking at you, Practical types) know at our cores that the state of our space affects us. We believe that objects have energy, both individually and collectively. What we surround ourselves with impacts how we feel, our state of mind, and our self-talk.

When we cultivate space and calm in our homes, we cultivate space and calm in our thoughts, our internal dialogue. This is due not only to the newly blank walls and clear surfaces, but also to the fact that in order to create a calm and peaceful home, a slowing down is required. Decluttering is a process of gaining clarity. Every time you decide to keep or let go of an item, you are effectively saying, "This matters to me" or

"This is no longer a priority." By decluttering an entire home, you have now made this decision hundreds of times. Looking around your new space, it ought to reflect the self that is most important to you, your deepest-held values.

THE HABIT OF RELEASING

This purge, when done deeply and honestly, means you will never need to do such a deep purge again. Think of this big decluttering event as a dietary cleanse: a full clearing out and a chance to start fresh. So it won't serve you to go back to eating junk food right away. All your hard work would be for naught. Instead, powerfully embody this refreshed energy and use this as a time to turn over a new leaf for good.

The hard work was parting with the old and breaking stubborn habits, and thus new habits must emerge in their place. In order for your home to retain its newly refreshed state, you must adopt these two crucial habits: releasing and mindful buying.

The first practice, to cultivate the habit of releasing, is part mental and part logistical. The mental portion is continuing to view the items in your life through an objective lens, taking note of when they no longer serve you. For example, if you realize you've tried on a shirt and decided against wearing it several times because it just doesn't fit right, take action then and there and place it in a bag destined for your local donation center. Don't simply put the item back in your closet.

The logistical portion requires creating a designated space in your home where these donations can be gathered and ensuring that you actually drop the items off at the donation center. A central yet out-of-the-way spot to keep a paper bag or bin for donations is the bottom of a hall or coat closet. Then find a drop-off location along one of your regular weekly routes that accepts a variety of belongings, such as Goodwill. This will ensure that all your items can go into one bag and that you are not creating more work for yourself by necessitating trips to multiple donation centers.

MINDFUL BUYING

The second most important habit is to completely reframe your shopping brain. Shopping becomes a reflexive habit when it's treated as a hobby or a way to kill time, connect with friends, reward oneself, or deal with an emotional struggle. This idea of shopping as an activity, a pastime, is something that both Cary and Kyle grew up understanding. After taking stock and decluttering our own lives, our current perspective on shopping could not be more different. We do not shop out of boredom; in fact, we avoid malls, fashion magazines, and other things that make people subconsciously feel the need to buy. Now when we have to buy something, we purchase only the items that we know are very important or needed in our lives.

Our favorite thing to hear from past clients (aside from that they're loving their amazing "new" home) is that the challenging decluttering process has totally changed how they look at things. When they are out and about in the world, the thoughts of "That's cute" or "That's a lovely color" or "It's on sale" or "I might need it" no longer precipitate a purchase. Instead, they can appreciate the item without physically needing to own it. They make lists and stick to them or take a long break from nonessential shopping altogether.

PURCHASE QUALITY GOODS

Of course, we acknowledge that there will be times in your life when you need to purchase something. Whether it's furniture or clothing or toys, we have one small, simple suggestion: purchase quality goods.

It takes time and energy to obtain something of quality, whether it involves saving up cash, seeking out the secondhand version, or coming up with a creative DIY alternative. This extra effort alone is a powerful determinant for whether having this item is actually a priority or is just a passing desire.

Furthermore, buying quality, well-made goods is actually the most effective way you can reduce consumption. It doesn't just slow the cycle of disposable items we've grown accustomed to—it removes the need for a cycle of consumption altogether.

Buying quality goods means that you will have them for a long time, maybe for life. If you do decide to replace a well-made item, a number of people can own this same item before or after you. This decreases the demand for new items, meaning that fewer items will be produced.

Additionally, using your hard-earned dollars toward purchasing quality goods bucks the trend of buying cheap items made from particleboard, cardboard, and cheap wood, which often end up in the landfill in just a few years.

On a deeper level, it feels amazing to be surrounded by thoughtfully produced things that were made with durability and craftsmanship in mind. There is a luxuriousness that comes from a worn leather couch (whether you've worn it in over the past forty years yourself or purchased it from someone else) that you simply can't get from a new polyester couch with toxic stuffing.

Rapid-fire purchasing also means we often tire of items, even if they have not fallen apart yet. You don't have to spend much time considering or planning for an object that is cheap to purchase and you expect to be rid of in a couple of months or years. It's a commitment to seek out and purchase well-made items, but it is worth it. When you take the time to really discern what you love and commit to finding a quality item meant to last, your home will feel that much more grounded, unique, and intentional.

JUST THE RIGHT AMOUNT

As we close, we return to New Minimalism's guiding light for thinking about our stuff: *lagom*. This word is a lens through which you can view each object you own, as well as a tool for creating your ideal calendar and honing your personal obligations. It's the Goldilocks theory. Find the amount of stuff or obligations that is "just right" for you—meaning the amount that suits you, supports you, and brings you joy.

Lagom is the luxurious, independently determined, optimistic version of "enough." It's softer, more fluid. It's one's personal best fit. For a passionate cake maker, a full baking set might be *lagom*, whereas for someone who prefers to patronize a local bakery for pastries and other sweet goodies, a simple baking pan might be enough. It's about being highly selective yet feeling abundant within the choices you make.

Rather than being burdened by our things, rather than putting our faith in stuff to make us happy, fulfilled, and complete, New Minimalism seeks out meaning in relationships, in the outdoors, in giving back, and in working toward goals you believe in. Useful and beloved items add to the joy and beauty of life. The key is to find a balance that is "just right," where your home and things support your pursuit of your best life—nothing more, nothing less.

RESOURCES

No matter where in the world you live, there are likely several organizations that will gratefully accept your donations. Below are suggestions for the types of organizations that we've found can accept specific items. To save yourself an extra trip, call ahead to find out if items are currently being accepted by your local organizations.

- **Clothing:** Most towns have donation organizations that will take your gently used clothing (popular US organizations include Goodwill and the Salvation Army).

- **Books:** Many local public libraries accept donations of books and other media. If the books are educational or child friendly, local schools and daycares will often gladly accept them as well.

- **Wedding dresses:** Brides Across America (www.bridesacross america.com) gifts wedding dresses to military brides. While based in Massachusetts, they accept mailed donations from around the country.

- **Women's professional clothing:** Dress for Success is a global organization that accepts donations throughout the world. These clothes empower and appropriately dress women for interviews and new jobs as they attain financial independence.

- **Furniture:** Some local secondhand stores as well as certain Goodwill and Salvation Army locations not only accept donations of furniture and home goods, but also provide free pick up of your furniture. The service and phone app Nextdoor (www.nextdoor .com) can be a great resource to give away items to your direct neighbors.

- **Unexpired food:** Local soup kitchens and homeless shelters typically accept donations of this kind.

- **Art supplies and office supplies:** Preschools and elementary schools are often in need of creative supplies.

- **Unopened toiletries, first aid, and beauty:** Local churches, homeless centers, or women's centers are often in need of these supplies for the communities they serve.

COMPOSTING TRICKS

If you are lucky enough to enjoy municipal composting provided by your city, you have no excuse! Please take advantage of this amazing service.

- To avoid stinky food scraps in the kitchen, use a brown paper bag or plastic salad-greens container to collect your compost in the freezer. Or, if you are making a large meal with lots of scraps, use a plastic bowl to collect the compost as you cook and clean, then dump in your outside container at the end of the night.
- The easiest way to compost in your own backyard is "cold composting": alternating layers of food scraps and yard trimmings in a bin to slowly decompose.
- If you're a serious gardener or inspired to take on a more active project, there are two other options: "vermicomposting" (composting with worms) and "aerated windrow composting" (composting that requires you periodically turn it over to incorporate oxygen).

RECYCLING

Reference the website of your waste-removal company, or call their hotline to learn what items they do or do not accept for recycling. For items that aren't included in your pick up (like glass bottles, in some cities), facilities do exist that can accept these items, but they often require you drop them off. Note: warm, fuzzy feelings ensue after making these earth-friendly efforts.

- **Plastic bags:** Most recycling facilities do not accept plastic bags because they clog the machines. Some grocery stores provide free drop-off locations for plastic-bag recycling.
- **Light bulbs (CFL), batteries, and paint:** most hardware stores will accept and properly dispose of these items for you.
- Use Recyclewhere.org to look up how to recycle pretty much anything else.

PHILOSOPHY BOOKS	*A New Earth* by Eckhart Tolle
	Becoming Wise by Krista Tippett
	Essentialism by Greg McKeown
	Simplicity Parenting by Kim John Payne
	Stuff: Compulsive Hoarding and the Meaning of Things by Randy Frost and Gail Steketee
	The Untethered Soul by Michael Singer
	When Breath Becomes Air by Paul Kalanithi
	Your Money or Your Life by Vicki Robin, Joe Dominguez, and Monique Tilford
PHILOSOPHY WEBSITES	Becoming Minimalist: www.becomingminimalist.com
	The Minimalists: www.theminimalists.com
	Zen Habits: www.zenhabits.net
SIMPLE WARDROBES	Project 333: www.theproject333.com
	Shira Gill: www.shiragill.com
	The Truth About Style by Stacy London
	Unfancy: www.un-fancy.com
ENVIRONMENT/ SUSTAINABILITY	*The Big Tiny* by Dee Williams
	"Leverage Points: Places to Intervene in a System" by Donella Meadows
	No Impact Man by Colin Beavan
	The Story of Stuff by Annie Leonard
	Zero Waste Home by Bea Johnson
DESIGN BOOKS	*Decorating with Style* by Abigail Ahern
	The Kinfolk Home by Nathan Williams
	Simple Matters by Erin Boyle
	SoulSpace by Xorin Balbes
DESIGN WEBSITES	Apartment Therapy: www.apartmenttherapy.com
	Coco Lapine: www.cocolapinedesign.com
	Design*Sponge: www.designsponge.com
	Jessica Helgerson: www.jhinteriordesign.com/residential
	My Scandinavian Home: www.myscandinavianhome.com
	Nicole Hollis: www.nicolehollis.com

ACKNOWLEDGMENTS

To our parents for teaching us what home means, for showing us how to live deep and meaningful lives, and for supporting us unconditionally on this long and winding road. If we could choose our families all over again, we'd choose you.

To our siblings, our best friends, for their humor and constant belief in us.

To our dearest friends for being absurdly supportive during this great experiment. Thank you for the wine and the late nights, and for being our sounding boards.

To Cam, this book, this career, this life, would all still be a dream if not for you.

To our canine companions, Bodhi and Dolly Walker, for being the world's snuggliest terriers.

To the brilliant, kind, and wise Hannah Elnan. You believed in this project and us before we did. We're grateful to you and the entire Sasquatch team for your passion, creativity, and commitment. It's an honor.

And finally, to our clients. Our deepest gratitude for letting us into your homes and inspiring us with your stories. It's your curiosity, generosity, and openness that make our work a joy and made this book possible. We adore you.

CHAPTER NOTES

PART I: THE
PHILOSOPHY

*Chapter 1: Laying the
Foundation*

On the decreased consumption of goods after the
   Industrial Revolution, see:
The Poverty of Affluence by Paul Wachtel

On the creation of the multimedia advertising industry, see:
"What Caused the Advertising Industry Boom in the 1950s?"
   by Valerie Bolden-Barrett in the *Houston Chronicle*
   (smallbusiness.chron.com/caused-advertising
   -industry-boom-1950s-69115.html)

On neuroscience and advertising, see:
"Marketers' Next Trick: Reading Buyers' Minds" by
   Kristen Schweizer in *Bloomberg Businessweek*
   (www.bloomberg.com/news/articles/2015-07-02
   /advertisers-use-neuroscience-to-craft-consumer-messages)

On leverage points, see:
"Leverage Points: Places to Intervene in a System"
   by Donella Meadows, 1997

On saving 71 percent of one's income, see:
www.frugalwoods.com/2015/01/09/well-hot-damn-frugality
   -works-our-2014-savings-rate-revealed

On not producing any trash, see:
www.zerowastehome.com/about/bea

On retiring at age thirty, see:
www.mrmoneymustache.com/2013/02/22
   /getting-rich-from-zero-to-hero-in-one-blog-post

On Peter Walsh's definition of *clutter*, see:
www.oprah.com/spirit/Peter-Walshs-Secrets
   -to-Cleaning-Up-Mess-and-Clutter

On the number of items in the average US household, see:
"For Many People, Gathering Possessions Is Just the Stuff of Life"
by Mary MacVean in the *Los Angeles Times*, March 21, 2014
(articles.latimes.com/2014/mar/21/health
/la-he-keeping-stuff-20140322)

On mortality and following your heart, see:
www.ted.com/talks/steve_jobs_how_to_live_before_you_die

Chapter 2:
The Decluttering Mind-Set

On setting boundaries for children, see:
Simplicity Parenting by Kim John Payne

Chapter 3: The Archetypes

On fear and the lizard brain, see:
Linchpin: Are You Indispensable? by Seth Godin

On cleaning out the garage, see:
www.becomingminimalist.com/5-years-of-better

On saying no, see:
How to Say "No" by Alexandra Franzen (www.alexandrafranzen
.com/wp-content/uploads/2017/01/how-to-say-no_free
-workbook_franzen.pdf)

On hoarding and trauma, see:
Stuff: Compulsive Hoarding and the Meaning of Things
by Randy O. Frost and Gail Steketee

Chapter 4:
Decluttering
+ Design

On clutter attracting more clutter, see:
www.westphoria.sunset.com/2015/11/16
/sunsets-great-clutter-challenge/

On storing your clothes in dry-cleaning bags, see:
www.abcnews.go.com/Business/busted-dry-cleaning-myths-wrong
/story?id=22785180#3

PART II: THE PRACTICE

Chapter 5: The Process	On dressing for yourself, see: *The Truth About Style* by Stacy London
Chapter 6: Category by Category	On more choices giving us less freedom, see: *The Paradox of Choice* by Barry Schwartz

On the ten-item wardrobe, see:
https://dailyconnoisseur.blogspot.com/2011/02/10-item-wardrobe
-getting-started.html

On hypercleanliness and health, see:
https://www.washingtonpost.com/national/health
-science/hypercleanliness-may-be-making-us
-sick/2013/03/25/9e6d4764-84e9-11e2-999e-5f8e0410cb9d
_story.html?utm_term=.0a8849b4edc3

On the endowment effect, see:
www.bigthink.com/insights-of-genius/rethinking-the-endowment
-effect-how-ownership-effects-our-valuations

On paying attention to how items make you feel, see:
The Desire Map by Danielle LaPorte

Chapter 7:
The Design Principles

On the Berlin supermarket Original Unverpackt, see:
www.theguardian.com/sustainable-business/2014/sep/16
/berlin-duo-supermarket-no-packaging-food-waste

On our ability to cherish only a limited number of things at
one time, see:
The Life-Changing Magic of Tidying Up by Marie Kondo

On electronics interfering with sleep, see:
Sleep Smarter by Shawn Stevenson

On cultivating a morning routine, see:
www.mymorningroutine.com

INDEX

Note: Photographs are indicated by *italics*.

A

advertising campaigns, 12–13
air quality, 158, *159*
archetypes, 35–57, 91
  See also specific archetype
authors' story, 3–6, *4*

B

beauty products. *See* toiletries
bed, storage bins under, 66
bedroom, removing electronics from, 164–166, *165*
bins, under-the-bed, 66
bring your own jar (BYOJ), 100
bulk, buying in, 154–155, *155*
busyness, cycle of, 116–119
buying habits. *See* shopping

C

category-by-category approach, 74–75
charity donations. *See* donations
children, 24–27, *25–26*, 62, 99, *162*, 163–164
choice, myth of, 91–92
cleaners, recipes for, 113
cleaning supplies and toiletries, 106–115, *108*, *114*
cleanliness, fixation on, 107, 109
closet, 62
  built-in system for, 151–152, *152*
  putting your dresser in, *150*, 151

See also wardrobe and accessories
clutter, definition of, 14–15
collections, 134–135
composting, 156, 186
Connected archetype, 39–42, 91, 131
consumerism, vii–viii, 12–14, 91–92
  See also shopping
container, bring your own, 100

D

dead space, 156–158, *157*
decluttering, reasons for, viii–xi, 18–19, 27, 29, 48–49
decluttering mind-set, 21–32
  See also New Minimalism
decluttering process, 73–89
  assistant, help from, 80–81, 83, 86
  category-by-category approach, 74–75, *76–77*
  "loving" your things, 78–79
  maintenance *versus* hitting the reset button, 16
  versus organization, 6–7, *7*, 10, 14
  preparing for, 80–82
  refraining from new purchases during, 30, 59–60
  step-by-step approach, 82–89
  time commitment, 80
  See also donations; New Minimalism; *specific category*